SCHOLASTIC INC.
New York Toronto London Auckland Sydney

ISBN 0-590-32170-6

12 11 10 9 8 7 6 5 0 1/9

Printed in the U.S.A. 01

One

Cheating the Gravedigger

This book is about a very strange kind of death, the kind that is supposed to happen, but doesn't. We all know that people are only just so strong, so tough. No one is supposed to survive, for example, jumping out of an airplane without a parachute and falling thousands of feet to the ground. We know that. But one man did. No one can survive weeks stranded in the middle of the frozen Antarctic with no shelter and little food, but one group of explorers did. And as you will soon know, absolutely no one is ever supposed to have walked away from his own execution, but somehow a few people did.

One of the big mysteries of life is: Why do some people manage to survive almost anything? The reasons vary. It might be a matter of skill, knowing just what to do when you have death staring you in the face. It might be a matter of determination, beating all the odds against survival by just believing that you're going to make it. It might be a matter of pure luck, sitting in one seat in a doomed airplane rather than another, or just making that one more step that takes you back from the edge of disaster to survival. Sometimes it might be a combination of all of these.

Whatever the reasons, the stories of how people manage to cheat death are endlessly fascinating and sometimes hair-raising as well. What this book offers you are some of the most chilling, weird, and sometimes even funny ways that people have managed to sidestep the one thing that all of us fear and dread the most—death.

As a young boy Dr. Jacques Winslow, a famous doctor in 18th-century Paris, had two strange confrontations with death that changed him for the rest of his life. They involved something called premature burial.

In his time doctors were not as well informed as they are now about how the human body works, and sometimes a doctor thought someone was dead when in fact the person was just unconscious. When this happened, people would occasionally put the unconscious person in a coffin and even bury him. Later, he would wake to find himself in a pitch-dark wooden box several feet below the earth and, unless some passing gravedigger heard the screams from the coffin, the person *would* die there.

For a long time people were terrified of this happening to them. And for good reason. Sometimes the only test a doctor made to see if someone was dead was to prick him with a pin. To avoid being prematurely buried, some stories went, rich people had special coffin rooms built where they would be laid to rest. These were equipped with a special coffin whose lid popped open at the touch of a finger. They often had windows and breathing tubes installed as well, and some rooms were even equipped with a few weeks' supply of food and water. Several stories have been written about the idea. Probably the most famous is Edgar Allan Poe's *The Fall of the House of Usher*, which is about a family that is subject to spells of deep, deathlike sleep. (The main character in the story accidentally buries his sister alive, mistaking one of her deep sleeps for death.)

Dr. Winslow had his own brush with death during an epidemic that swept through his village when he was a child. Thousands of people were sick with a mysterious illness that moved across France. Many of them died. Young Winslow himself came down with the illness and at one point he slipped into unconsciousness.

Mistaking this for death, his parents brought him to a central burial place. The custom in those days was to bury the dead as quickly as possible to prevent infection. This time, however, they did it too quickly.

Because of his fever Winslow didn't remember slipping into unconsciousness, but he certainly remembered waking up. When he opened his eyes he was lying in a narrow box in a large room. Raising his head up he looked over the edge and saw dozens of other boxes like his. In each was someone who had died. He screamed and shouted when he realized where he was. In a few minutes some terrified cemetery workers timidly peeked in to see who or what was screaming. They were relieved to see it was just a live boy and not some ghoul.

As if that wasn't terrifying enough, approximately a year later Winslow once again fell ill and lapsed into a coma. Remembering their last mistake the family did the medical tests to make sure the boy was dead. They pricked him with a pin. He showed no sign of feeling it, as would anyone in a coma. So once again they gave up his body for burial and once again Winslow woke up to the horror of being in a room full of dead people.

Not surprisingly these experiences marked him for the rest of his life, and when he became a doctor one of the things that fascinated him most in medicine was death, or more specifically how to tell when a person has genuinely died. He wrote a famous book on the subject, *The Uncertainty of the Signs of Death and the Danger of Precipitate Interments and Dissections*, and he pleaded with other doctors to be more cautious before sending their patients off to the graveyard.

As part of his work he helped start the whole idea of the mortuary, storing bodies for a short time, usually about three days, before burying them to prevent a premature burial. In fact, eventually there were laws passed requiring that no one be buried until this waiting period had passed.

In the 1700s, when Winslow was in Paris, a typical mortuary was a bizarre place to visit. The one in Paris, for example, looked like a miniature prison. Each body was stored in its own locked room. Guards patrolled the corridors outside the rooms on a steady schedule. Their job was to look in on the corpses to see if anyone happened to wake up. Sometimes doctors also went around with the guards to check up on the dead.

In every cell the body was laid out on a stone slab and on one of its hands there was a glove. That had a string tied around the tip of one of its fingers and the string was connected to a bell. The slightest movement of the body would set the bell clanging and bring the guard running. If anyone did suddenly awaken in one of these rooms, he could be rushed to a pharmacy that was specially equipped to revive the person. In time, as doctors gained more skill in figuring out who was really dead and who wasn't, this kind of mortuary faded from use. But it did save some lives and would never have existed if it hadn't been for the French boy who had almost been buried alive, twice.

It is possible to understand how there could be some confusion about death since there are conditions that closely resemble it; but it's hard to believe that someone's death sentence can be handed down in a court of law, that the execution be set for a certain date, that the execution even be carried out . . . and that the condemned criminal lives to walk away, or in some instances run away.

One of the earliest examples of this was the 17th-century case of an English woman named Anne Greene. She was tried for murder and, even though the evidence seemed to indicate she was innocent, the aristocratic family for whom she worked was convinced she was guilty and used its influence to persuade the court.

The persuasion worked. The court decided that

Anne was guilty of murder and condemned her to death by hanging at Oxford. There was next to no chance she would ever get a reprieve from the court and she knew it. So to make her death as quick and as painless as possible she asked her friends to pull down hard on her body to get the hanging over with quickly.

The grim day arrived, and as she expected, with no reprieve in sight. It was a bitter cold December morning as she marched up to the scaffold where the hangman stood ready with his rope. She waited patiently as the priest read prayers off to one side and the hangman gently lowered the noose over her head and tightened it. The prayers done, and with nothing more to say about the injustice being done to her, Anne Greene stood there bravely as the floor dropped away beneath her and she swung to her death. Her friends did as she had asked. They pulled down to make the agony as brief as possible, and after she had been hanging for half an hour, Anne was cut down and her body carried off to doctors who needed it for dissections.

It is hard to say who was more surprised, the doctor or the "corpse" he had laid out in front of him. Shortly after Anne Greene's body was delivered to the doctor's dissecting room a bizarre thing happened. He was just about to make the first incision with his surgical knife when he thought the body moved. He hesitated and watched. It moved again.

Anne Greene was still very much alive, much to her own surprise and joy and that of her friends. When she was completely revived by the doctors, they sent word back to the court that their executed murderess was still very much alive.

The court was so impressed it gave Anne Greene what she had originally hoped for, a total reprieve. She lived on to marry and have three children and enjoy a long, happy life.

About eighty years later another convicted murderess, this one named Margaret Dixon, had a similar resurrection in Scotland in 1728. As with Anne Greene, Dixon was condemned to be hanged, and to satisfy the law the woman was duly executed at Musselburgh in Scotland at the hand of a professional hangman. After hanging the required amount of time she was cut down and laid out in a coffin. Gravediggers were carrying her to the cemetery in the open coffin and took a route that wound through town. The execution had caused some excitement in the town, customers at a local inn stepped outside to get a look at the grim procession passing by. As it turned out, they got a little more excitement than they had bargained for.

The gravediggers were passing the inn when they felt the coffin shift around. Looking up they saw the executed and supposedly dead Margaret Dixon sitting up, trying to climb out. A local reporter on the scene mentioned that the curious customers from the inn were "greatly scared" when they saw what they thought was a dead woman sit up.

As it happened, under Scottish law Dixon was officially dead. She had been hanged as the law demanded, and as far as any judge was concerned, she was executed. The fact that she didn't actually die at the hands of the official hangman was beside the point.

Naturally this made Mrs. Dixon very, very happy but it did complicate her life a little bit. Since she was officially dead, her husband was also, officially, a widower. She could not go back home and live with a man to whom she was no longer married, the strict Scottish laws said, until she wed her husband a second time. She did, and became his second as well as his first wife.

Modern criminals have not always made out as well when their time came. Back in the 1930s a convicted murderer known only by the name of Bullen had been sentenced to death in the electric chair at Sing Sing prison in New York. In due time Bullen was marched down Death Row to the room where the deadly chair was kept. He was strapped in, and on a signal, thousands of volts of electricity went surging through his body.

After the execution, Bullen's body was put in a crude prison coffin and carried out toward the prisoners' cemetery where others were buried. On the way, Bullen proved that he was a tough man to execute. He woke up, and managed to kick open the top of the coffin. Then he ran for freedom. Since he was still inside the prison grounds, he didn't get very far. The guards caught him, put him back in his cell, and, unlike the others mentioned here, he got no reprieve. A few weeks later he was strapped to the same electric chair and shortly afterward made his second and last trip to the cemetery where he is today.

Not all modern execution stories end the same way. Some have what you might call a happy ending. For example, a few years ago, in 1973, two gangsters decided it was time to murder an informer, or stool pigeon, named Vinny Ensulo (also known as Vinnie Ba Ba Vincent Ennisie). They were cruising around Brooklyn in a car when they spotted him walking down the street. Jumping out, they made him get in the back seat. Each had a gun and each was pointing it straight at the head of Vinnie Ba Ba. Things did not look promising.

But while they were sitting there with Vinnie between them the car suddenly swerved to avoid an enormous pothole in the street. The two gangsters, who had already had nervous trigger fingers, fired their pistols. Unfortunately for them the swerve of the car threw Vinnie down on the floor so that when they pulled the triggers there was no one and nothing between them. As a result they shot each other. Vinnie got away.

Another attempted murder that didn't come off for different reasons all began with a woman named Hildie Kleiner, a headache, and a train ride. Mrs. Kleiner was traveling through West Germany in 1948 when she met a man riding in her train compartment who identified himself as a doctor. Dr. Berger, he called himself. All of her life the woman had suffered from blinding headaches. She asked the doctor if he knew of any cure that could help her. As it happened, he did. He was a specialist in hypnosis and had years of experience treating many different kinds of medical problems with it. He gave her his card and invited her to come to his office in Heidelberg for treatment.

A short time later she visited him, and her headaches did disappear. She also had other ailments she wanted him to treat with this wonderful hypnotic technique. She began visiting him first one, then two, three, even four times each week. And each time she paid a visit he put her under hypnosis, but not only for medical reasons.

It was about this time that Mrs. Kleiner tried to do a bizarre and unexpected thing. She tried to murder her husband, whom she loved. The first time she tried to kill him with some rat poison. One night as she was preparing dinner she mixed a large spoonful of the deadly stuff in with a stew she was making. Her husband ate heartily that night, but later on complained of an upset stomach. He felt an awful ache. That passed in a few hours, and he was feeling fine once again.

The following night the woman stirred two huge spoons of the poison into the batter of a cake she was making. It was her husband's favorite, chocolate. That night he had extras on dessert. He also felt a little sick later on and was up most of the night. By morning he was feeling much better. He suspected all that rich cake was too much for his digestive system.

Mrs. Kleiner decided to try one last time. She roasted a chicken with some special stuffing in it just for her husband. It had three spoonfuls of rat poison in it. Within minutes after leaving the table the man felt horribly sick. He couldn't hold anything down, not even a sip of water. The pain he felt was excruciating. Until dawn the next day he paced the house continually trying to fight off this spectacular attack of indigestion. And he did. Miraculously he had survived a triple dose of rat poison.

From then on he seemed to be accident-prone. He was out on his motorcycle one day when his brakes suddenly and mysteriously failed. Fortunately, he wasn't going too fast and was thrown clear. The mechanic who later worked on the motorcycle said the brakes were in fine shape but the cables controlling them weren't. They had neatly snapped in two, almost as if someone had deliberately cut them. Someone had — Mrs. Kleiner.

A few weeks later the man decided to repair the steep roof on his house. He had gotten a ladder, climbed up onto the roof, and was halfway across the top when his foot suddenly slipped. He tried to regain his balance with the other foot, but that slipped too. He was skidding backward toward the edge of the roof and the forty-foot drop that waited beyond it. He clawed out with his hands to get some sort of grip. They were useless. There was a slimy coating on the roof's shingles. It was oil. Somehow a huge slick of oil had been poured across the section of the roof where he planned to work. There was nothing to hold on to. He kept slipping back. He went over the edge.

As he did, he made one last lunge and just by chance his hand caught the edge of the gutter. The ladder had disappeared. He wasn't sure, but he thought he saw his wife pull it away. There was one last chance. Using all his strength he worked his way over to a corner drainpipe and shimmied down to the ground. His knees were shaking when he landed.

Part of the story behind his "accidents" seemed to involve the new doctor. Ever since his wife had been going to Dr. Berger strange things had been happening. First the household money disappeared. Then money from their savings account gradually diminished. And then after he had complained to the police about his suspicions that Dr. Berger was somehow filching money from his wife, these accidents started.

What Mr. Kleiner, or even Mrs. Kleiner, had no way of knowing at the time was that Dr. Berger was using hypnosis to give certain commands to Mrs. Kleiner. Berger, for example, told the woman to bring him all of her household money. After she did that, he told her to start bringing what she had saved in the bank. At that point the husband went to the police. When Berger found out, he gave Mrs. Kleiner hypnotic instructions to kill her husband.

The police could do nothing. As it happened Dr. Berger, or whoever he really was, had devised the perfect protection. While he had Mrs. Kleiner under hypnosis he also instructed her to remember nothing at all about him once she was out of the trance; and although he had sent her several notes telling her how to kill her husband, he had also planted the command in her mind to burn the notes immediately after reading them. The conscious Mrs. Kleiner was of no help to the police. Even the hypnotized woman was no help at first.

She had been instructed by the clever doctor to respond only to his voice.

With patience and time a hypnotist hired by the police had been able to gradually break down the hypnotic wall Berger had built in Mrs. Kleiner's mind. Little by little he teased out scraps of information about the doctor: what his examination room looked like, the kinds of clothes he wore, small details about his office.

Hearing about the investigation, Berger got worried. He sent an accomplice to her house and tried to find out how much she had told the police. (He had even prepared for this by having hypnotized the woman to forget about anyone who came to her house in Dr. Berger's name.) There wasn't enough to worry about, Berger decided.

For the meantime the police agreed. They had a description of a man they couldn't find, who may or may not be a doctor and who, if caught, could not be arrested for anything. They had no connection between the doctor and the murder attempts on Mr. Kleiner's life.

Finally the police hypnotist tried a trick. He hypnotized the woman and handed her a blank slip of paper. He said it was a note from Dr. Berger and asked her to read it to him. Relying totally on her hypnotic memory, the woman read off the contents of one of the notes sent to her and then burned the blank slip of paper. The hypnotist handed her another blank note and asked her to read that one. Again from memory she read off another of Berger's messages. Working this way, the police uncovered the commands to murder the husband and, eventually, got a clear description of the doctor's accomplice. Armed with that description they went through their files and identified the man. From there it was a small step to find Dr. Berger.

The "doctor" turned out to be a swindler named Reinhold Heufling who had a police record for fraud, among other things. He denied he had ever met Mrs. Kleiner, much less that he hypnotized her to murder her husband. And there was no way, he said, the police could link her to him.

His story changed once the police started reading him Mrs. Kleiner's elaborate descriptions of his apartment, which included details such as the kinds of objects strewn across the top of his desk. The circumstantial evidence was enough to arrest the phony Dr. Berger, and get him a sentence of ten years in prison.

Ordinarily a prison sentence is just a temporary inconvenience for the hardened criminal, but there have been few prisons in the modern world that offered a death sentence of another kind, a living death. Probably the most famous in this century was the notorious Alcatraz, also known as The Rock.

Originally built in the 1800s as a fort, Alcatraz was periodically used as a prison over the years, mostly by the U.S. Army, but didn't really become a federal penitentiary until the 1930s. The U.S. government was looking for what is called a maximum security prison, basically an escape-proof building where it could lock up its most vicious and dangerous criminals. Alcatraz was the perfect place. Although it's on a small island only a few miles off the shore of California and a short distance away from San Francisco, what passes between that island and the coast are some of the most unpredictable and murderous tides possible. Anyone attempting to swim to shore stands a good chance of being ensnared by the tides and swept out to sea. The inside was almost as hostile as the outside. Each cell was four feet by eight feet, barely the size of a large closet. Furnishings were minimal — one chair, a desk, a fold-up bunk, and a sink; and so were comforts — food, clothing, a shower once a week, and the right to see the doctor if ill. Prisoners were allowed to talk for only six minutes each weekday and for two hours on weekends. Anyone caught breaking that and other rules was punished brutally by getting sent to the "hole," a solitary confinement cell with no furniture except a skimpy straw mattress that the guard took away every morning. The daily diet there was bread and water, with one real meal once every three days.

The strain of being locked in the pitch-black hole for days, weeks, or even months was more than some prisoners could stand both mentally and physically. Some men died there. Others came out wracked with pneumonia or crippled with arthritis. And still others emerged as babbling idiots, hopelessly insane prisoners who spent the rest of their days in a padded cell in the prison's hospital ward. Others committed suicide to end the horror of life at Alcatraz. Still others were willing to take the ultimate life or death risk and try to escape. Most lost.

But only five other convicts in the history of Alcatraz actually managed to break out and at least get as far as the San Francisco Bay waters. Whether or not they ever made it to shore, no one really knows. The authorities never found any bodies, and they believe that all the escapees were probably swept out to sea and drowned like all the others who had tried.

Still, the notoriously treacherous tides around Alcatraz are not always deadly. They are milder on some days than others, so it is possible that some men did get to shore but simply never were caught. According to those who have studied famous escapes from The Rock, if anyone could have successfully escaped, it was probably the 35-year-old convicted bank robber named Frank Lee Morris. Faced with a long jail sentence in that punishing place, Morris figured even the risk of drowning had to be a better alternative to Alcatraz. So, together with two other convicts, he began planning an escape.

The plan began with the air vents in their cells. Working with tools they made in the prison shop, the men gradually chipped away at the concrete until they hacked out an opening wide enough for a human body to crawl through. They stuffed the dust from the broken concrete into their pockets and dumped it in the prison yard during their outside work detail.

Work was painfully slow. Guards checked on the prisoners every hour so what work they did had to be accomplished in short spurts. To cover the large gaps in the wall, the men positioned sheets of cardboard, realistically painted to look like the air-vent grating, and put them over the holes. Just widening one hole took months; but Morris and his friends had all the time in the world.

The next part of the plan was to complain to the warden about the ceiling in their cell block. In fact it was flaking and disintegrating. It would help, suggested the convicts, if a sheet or blanket was hung under it to catch the paint and flakes of cement that constantly fell off. The warden agreed. Once a week, one of Morris's friends would go up to clean out the paint chips the blanket had collected. And, hidden from the sight of the guards, he would also gradually loosen the bolts holding the screening over the roof's air vent.

Finally, after months of preparation, Morris and his men were ready to move on June 12, 1962. They went through their daily routine and went to bed, as usual. The guards came by and took their hourly head count of the sleeping convicts. As usual everyone was there. But not really. Morris had his friend, who worked in the prison barber shop, save some hair clippings. These he glued to the head of a realistic dummy he and the other two convicts put in their bunks. When the guards came by at night they counted the dummies, not the men.

In the meantime, the real convicts had scrambled through the air vents and up through the loosened screen that opened onto the roof. Dodging searchlights, they scrambled across the rooftops of the prison, slipped over the walls, and climbed down to the rocks of San Francisco Bay. Once there, they inflated homemade swimming vests, cleverly made out of the sleeves of plastic raincoats sneaked out of the prison's clothes factory. With these inflated, they slipped into the water and pushed off.

It was nine hours before the guards realized their mistake. They sent out a warning and boats began sweeping the area for signs of the convicts. No trace of them was ever found except for a wallet belonging to one of the convicts. It had washed up on shore north of San Francisco. A manhunt was on all over the country, but police never turned up another sign of the men. The authorities decided the men had drowned.

Others are not so convinced. For one thing the usually strong tides were very mild that night, so even a mediocre swimmer with a good swim vest could have crossed the distance to the mainland without a great struggle. Also Morris was a shrewd, intelligent planner who seemed to think of everything. Many believe that the wallet was just a decoy to throw police off the scent and make them think the men had drowned. Finally, it does seem likely that someone who had planned as long and as carefully as Morris had would also have equally detailed plans for staying hidden once he escaped. He had friends on the outside who could have helped, and maybe did. Who is to say that somewhere in the United States Frank Lee Morris lives, by another name of course, and that every so often he flies out to San Francisco to take a one-day sightseeing boat trip out to the now abandoned Alcatraz, just for old time's sake?

Two

Law of the Jungle

In cities and towns it's the law of the people that rule how we live, but as soon as we leave those places behind and move into the wilderness a whole new law takes over. That law is survival, no matter what the cost. In the jungles, in the forests, in the mountains, in all the wild places on earth, this law applies equally to every living thing. People are no exceptions. Even with all of our brains and our sophisticated weapons, there are times when "dumb" animals, following the law of survival, are more than a match for humans. This is especially true if an animal is one of that rare but deadly breed of beasts, the man-killer.

Every so often it will happen that animals which usually avoid humans mysteriously change their habits and not only lose their fear of people, but start to hunt them down and kill them. Why a supposedly normal animal becomes a man-killer has mystified scientists and animal experts for decades. Sometimes the animal kills people because it was raised that way and has always thought of people as food. Sometimes an animal is too old and slow to catch other animals and settles on going after the comparatively slow-moving human. And sometimes the animal may become a mad killer for no apparent reason.

Among African animals few have the reputation of the shrewd, treacherous Cape buffalo. These are large, horned animals, weighing a little less than a ton. They have the most unpredictable and, some hunters say, the most vicious temperament of all of Africa's big game. Bulls, especially those that avoid the herds and travel alone, are the most feared. These wander about in the thick bush where they sometimes spring out and surprise some poor unwary human, and try to spear him with their sharp curved horns.

One of the really unnerving features of the animals is that they will charge a human with no warning or provocation. They have also been more than a match for some hunters, as they will casually move out of rifle range of the person stalking them and travel in a large circle until they can come up from behind and attack. Then, as one wildlife expert put it, "There is one merciful thing about being killed by a buffalo: death is usually instant."

The Cape buffalo when angry is almost impossible to stop. The heavy horn on the top of its head and its thick skull are practically bulletproof, and even if a hunter should shoot one fatally, the Cape buffalo won't always cooperate by dying, at least not right away. One hunter fired what he was certain was a deadly shot at the buffalo and was horrified to see it still keep running straight at him. After the animal covered almost two hundred yards, it finally fell dead at his feet.

As vicious and deadly as its attack usually is, there are people who have survived it and lived to tell. One was an African honey-gatherer named William Kibet. While walking through the tall grass on his way to a beehive, he literally stumbled over a sleeping buffalo. The animal woke with a quick head shake that caught the man with the tip of its horn and threw him up in the air. The terrified man came falling down on the back of the bull.

Not knowing what happened, the bull took off with the man hugging his back and clinging to one of the bull's ears. Paralyzed with terror, the man hung on for as long as he could until the bull went running under a low-hanging tree branch. That knocked the rider off his back and onto the ground, where he was completely helpless. Wheeling around, the Cape buffalo charged again, stabbing the man with a horn as he passed. Satisfied with his conquest, the buffalo wandered off leaving his victim for dead.

Lying as still as possible, Kibet waited until he was certain the buffalo had gone. He was hurt badly. One hand was broken and he was bleeding heavily from the bull's goring. Fortunately there was a small creek close by. Inch by inch Kibet managed to crawl over to it. Slowly, carefully, using his good hand, he poured the cool water over his injuries and took a long drink. Barely able to move, he had to stay by that stream out in the wild. Animals wandered by the stream to drink — lions, hyenas, elephants — and miraculously none of them even took a second look at the wounded man. One day went by, two days, a whole week, then another week. By the end of the second week some other honey-gatherers came wandering by. He heard their voices and called out weakly. They didn't believe what they saw. They had given him up for dead days ago. They had already seen the blood, the buffalo tracks, and had figured that he had been killed and that animals had carried off his body. Kibet finally made it back to his village, two weeks late, but alive.

Others have survived the deadly buffalo in even better shape. There was the South African hunter, Tobi Rochat, who was out hunting when out of the brush came charging what he thought was certain death: a Cape buffalo, its head and horns held low. He turned to grab his rifle, which was held by his gunbearer, but when he reached for it, it was not there. Neither was the gunbearer. The man had simply run away in fear. Unarmed and standing right in the path of the bull, Rochat knew it was over. Without even the chance of a shot he was a dead man. The bull came bearing down and rammed Rochat hard, pushing the man back against a dense bush. Digging in his feet, the bull drove the man's body down toward the ground trying to pin him with its horns.

But each time he pushed the man sprang back up. The bush was acting as a kind of crude shock absorber, and it kept bouncing Rochat back at the frustrated bull. Again and again the bull rammed

Rochat. Again and again he popped back up. Totally exasperated, the bull finally gave up, leaving behind one flattened bush and one amazed and relieved human being.

Of all the animals best equipped to match wits with humans, it is generally agreed that no creature can come close to the tiger for its cunning and elusiveness. An almost silent and extremely clever hunter itself, the tiger moves like a shadow through the jungles of Asia as it stalks its prey. And among tigers there has probably been none as famous as the man-eater of Champawat. Before the animal was finally hunted down, it had by itself killed four hundred thirty-six people, the largest number of humans ever killed by a single cat.

The animal had started its human diet in Nepal in 1904 and, after eating two hundred thirty-six people there, it wandered over the border into northern India in search of more food. For three years it terrorized entire villages there to the point where farmers were afraid to walk into the fields to harvest the crops. Women were terrified of even going off to draw water. Mothers would not let their children play out of their sight. The animal terrified thousands because it didn't seem to be made of flesh and blood. Without warning it would move into an area and, with the deadly invisibility of an evil spirit, would carry off and eat someone. At night the fearful natives would hear the tiger roaring and were left to wonder who would be its next victim.

Finding this tiger, or for that matter finding any

tiger, was not an easy job. Tigers are solitary creatures that tend to wander over vast areas of land rather than stick to one part of the country. Experienced hunters tell of tigers wandering over a thousand miles without ever coming to the same place twice. Tigers generally avoid humans, and even in the days when they were not on the verge of extinction, they were seldom seen by people. The only ones people were most likely to come in contact with were the man-killers, like the Killer of Champawat.

It showed no fear of people and more than once was even seen calmly walking around carrying its latest human victim in its mouth. Also, many of its victims were believers in the Hindu religion, which holds that at least some remains of a deceased person have to be cremated before his soul will be admitted to heaven. Often the relatives of someone who was carried off by the tiger would go and try to find something of the victim to cremate. What then happened was that they became victims themselves.

In one particularly sad case, a woman and her sister were out working in the fields cutting grass when the tiger sprang from behind a bush. In a flash it killed the sister and began walking off with her body. Stunned to see her sister being dragged away by a wild beast, the woman chased after the animal trying to hit it with the small sickle she was carrying.

Without warning the tiger dropped the sister's body and wheeled to face the woman. With a spine-chilling roar it lunged, barely missing her.

Absolutely terrified at her brush with death, the woman dropped the sickle and ran back to her village. The whole experience of seeing her sister killed and nearly being killed herself had a strange effect on the poor woman. She became completely speechless. Whenever she opened her mouth in an attempt to explain what had happened, not a word came out, not a sound. She was still in that state when Jim Corbett arrived a year later.

Corbett, thirty-two years old, was a professional hunter who specialized in hunting down man-killing tigers, leopards, and lions. He had heard about the Killer of Champawat and had come to eliminate it. It was obvious from what he had learned about the cat that this was no ordinary man-eater. It definitely was not sick or old as some were. Most of those kinds of man-eaters were easily hunted down after killing one or two victims. This tiger had killed literally hundreds of people and already eluded some of the best hunters in the country. Corbett had made a mental note to himself to be extra wary so he wouldn't be another one on the tiger's long list of human meals.

He began his hunt by chasing down killings in the area. For a while each time he arrived at a place, the tiger was one step ahead. It had quickly killed and moved on. On one of many missed meetings with the killer, he ran into a group of terrified men. They had been walking on a ridge when they heard cries and screams. Looking down they saw, to their horror, the tiger walking along, carrying a live woman in his mouth as though she were a kitten. The woman pleaded for help but the men, who were unarmed, had to stand and watch helplessly as the large cat walked into the jungle with its latest victim.

Finally Corbett got lucky and arrived at a village just after the tiger had attacked a 16-year-old girl who had been out gathering firewood. By the time Corbett arrived at the spot, the tracks were still fresh. All that was left of the girl was a few beads from a broken necklace and a pool of blood. Carefully, Corbett followed the tracks until he came to the edge of a small pool. There he made a grim discovery, blood-stained shreds of the girl's clothing.

While he was looking at this, Corbett let his concentration slip and for a second totally forgot about the tiger. Some stones rolled down a hillside and splashed into the pond. Instinctively grabbing his rifle, he turned and aimed just in time to see the tiger pull its head down and walk away. It had been watching him all the time, but for some reason did not attack.

Corbett took off after it, slipping and stumbling over the rough, rocky ground that the tiger moved over so easily. Each time the animal paused to try to eat its victim, the young girl, Corbett would gain a little ground, but then the tiger would move on. Eventually the big cat wandered down into a valley so thick with brush and thorn bushes that Corbett couldn't follow. By then he had already worked out a plan to trap the man-killer.

There was only one way out of the valley, through a narrow pass. Corbett thought that if he could organize the village to form a line of people making noise by beating on kettles, firing guns, and doing anything to make a racket, they could drive the animal toward that pass. There, the hunter would be waiting for the kill.

The next day two hundred ninety-eight village men went marching through the valley making as much noise as they could and moving slowly toward the open end of the ravine. There, with two other villagers, Corbett waited. A few minutes went by when he thought he saw some brush move. Then out into a small clearing bounded the tiger, the Killer of Champawat. Slowly and deliberately Corbett raised his rifle and took careful aim. But before he could pull the trigger, two shots went off. One of the scared villagers next to him had fired his rusty old rifle and in his excitement not only missed the animal completely, but scared it back into the brush. Corbett tried a quick shot just before the tiger disappeared, but he missed. Once again it looked like the man-killer would escape.

This time the noisemakers made the difference between success and failure. Hearing the racket of the marching villagers even louder and closer than before, the tiger turned and ran back into the opening. This time Corbett was ready. He fired. The cat stopped dead in its tracks. Slowly it turned his head and glared at him. Quickly reloading, Corbett fired again. The shot would have killed any other tiger but for some reason the animal did not go down. It started to move away, back into the bush. Out of ammunition, Corbett grabbed an ancient rifle from the astonished man standing next to him and went into the bush after the tiger.

By then the animal had circled back and hopped up on a rocky ledge overlooking where Corbett now stood. When it saw him, the tiger moved slowly toward the hunter, stalking him. He turned to face the animal. The moment of truth had come. Corbett raised the old rifle and was about to fire, when he saw that there was a large crack in the end of the barrel. He was sure that if he pulled the trigger the bullet would backfire and explode in his face, blinding him. He was equally sure that if he did not shoot, he would be the tiger's next victim. He aimed, and pulled the trigger. The rifle kicked back hard but did not blow up. Slowly the tiger stepped forward and then fell dead. The terror was over.

When Corbett later examined the animal's body, he found what could have been the reason for its turning man-killer. An old gunshot wound had shattered what were probably once sharp canine teeth, essential for killing animals. Deprived of these, the animal turned to easier prey, people.

Later on, when the body of the man-killer was carried back to the village, the woman who had not spoken a word since the day it killed her sister looked up at the dead tiger and gave a shout of joy.

We, here in North America, don't have to worry about man-killing elephants or tigers, but we do have our share of dangerous animals. The grizzly bear is at least as formidable as the wild animals of the jungle. Try to picture an animal as big as a small car, weighing a quarter of a ton, and, in spite of all that weight, faster on four feet than man is on two. That is the grizzly bear, over five hundred pounds of powerful muscle with one of the keenest minds in the animal world.

Typically, the bear minds its own business and, unless it is a mother with cubs, travels by itself avoiding even other bears for company. It has a ravenous appetite and eats almost anything: berries, insects, small game, large animals such as deer, and if one is careless enough to cross its path, an occasional human.

The grizzly is as brave as it is smart. It fears nothing. Faced with what it thinks is a threat or danger, the grizzly will do just one thing, attack. And when man meets grizzly, it is usually the bear that walks away in one piece.

This was almost the case in the 1800s when a party of trappers had traveled up the Missouri River in search of animal furs. One of them was an experienced hunter named Hugh Glass. He was a man who seemed born to survive anything, including the Indian attack on his party that left fifteen of his companions dead. But even his luck seemed to run out the day he spotted a grizzly and shot it.

Instead of killing the bear, the bullet simply infuriated it. Moving with incredible speed the bear bounded through the brush after Glass who had already dropped his rifle and had begun climbing up a nearby tree. He had only gotten a few feet when the bear dug its claws into the man's back and by brute force dragged him out of the branches. Once it had Glass on the ground it began tearing at him with its powerful claws.

There were other hunters standing around with loaded rifles, but each was afraid to shoot in case he hit Glass by accident. Eventually the bear stopped mauling Glass's body and started to walk off. The hunters opened fire. Instead of running away the bear spun around and attacked Glass again. And the men had to stop shooting again. Soon it lost interest in the man on the ground, and it turned and walked away. Again the men started shooting. Somehow associating the bullets with the man on the ground, the bear turned and, for a third time, was about to swipe at the man when it was finally shot dead by the hunters. Its limp body fell on top of Glass.

Carefully the men rolled the huge animal's body off of Hugh Glass. Incredibly he was still breathing but very badly mauled. Judging by his wounds the men knew he wouldn't have much time left to live. Also the area was full of hostile Indians who may have heard the shooting, and they could not survive another Indian attack. They wanted to get out of there fast.

The leader of the group asked that someone stay behind and watch over Glass in his last moments. No one volunteered. The man then offered money to stay and two men named Tom Fitzpatrick and Sid Bridger said they would stay by the dying man.

They did, for two days. On the third day, Glass was still alive but he was fading fast. By then the men were even more nervous about Indians, so instead of waiting around to do the decent thing and bury Glass, they left him and went off to join the rest of the party and took Glass's rifle with them. The last time they saw him he was lying on the ground delirious and slipping in and out of a deep, deathlike trance. He looked like a dead man already.

But they had underestimated Hugh Glass. The day after they left he came out of his coma and, using what little strength he had, he dragged his torn body over to a cool mountain stream. Food came from nearby wild berry bushes. Too weak to move, Glass lay in that spot for almost two weeks slowly building up his strength. Once he felt able, he staggered to his feet and crawled off in the direction of Fort Kiowa, the nearest outpost, roughly one hundred miles away.

Weeks went by as he stumbled through the wild. Sometimes it took him a whole day to walk just a half mile. As his strength built up, he managed to walk longer and longer stretches. His luck finally began to change. While groping along, he was spotted by a small group of French hunters. They took him to the fort where he completed his recovery and managed to get some more supplies. As it happened the Frenchmen were heading up the Missouri River, exactly where Glass's party had gone. Not wanting to miss a chance at getting even with Fitzpatrick and Bridger, he headed upriver with them. While on the trip his luck almost changed again for the worse. A war party of Indians attacked his group.

Everyone in it was killed except for two men, a French trapper, and Hugh Glass.

After more days of backwoods traveling Glass found his original hunting party's camp. It had been months now since he shot that bear and been left to die, but to Glass it was as vivid as if it had happened that morning. He couldn't forget it. The tough old mountain man wanted revenge.

As he approached the camp, his mood began to mellow slightly seeing some old friends. Those who turned and saw him first went pale. Some were convinced it was a ghost and not the real Hugh Glass. He savored the look of shock on their faces, especially on those of Fitzpatrick and Bridger. As they stood there, with their mouths hanging open, their eyes fixed on him, Glass walked over and said just three words, "Where's my rifle?"

Three

Death from the Depths

Even today humans are strangers in the vast and still mysterious world of the sea. At best, we can only be visitors there. If we linger there too long we become intruders and, if we're not careful, somebody's next meal.

Although it is true that most creatures that live in the deep fear humans, there are exceptions. The most deadly exception is probably the shark. There are few animals worth fearing as much as a man-killing shark. It's a primitive creature. Its brain is small and the shark is not too bright. Its vision is not the best, either. However, it has other abilities that make up for these handicaps.

For one thing it has a keen sense of smell. It can pick up the scent of just a trace of blood in the water. For another, it has a kind of built-in sonar. Just underneath the skin on the sides of its body are rows of extremely sensitive nerves that can feel vibrations given off by a struggling fish, or a person in the water.

What propels the shark is its voracious appetite. It seems to have been born to do just two things: kill and eat. And it does both extremely well. It is so good at them that one shark expert had dubbed the creature "an eating machine."

In all there are two hundred fifty species of sharks. They vary in size, shape, and viciousness. Some, as far as people are concerned, are relatively harmless. Others are swift, powerful "eating machines" that seem to specialize in humans. Of these the most dangerous is the great white shark. It is too powerful to fear anything. There are stories about some of them attacking whole boats in a killing frenzy. And they are unpredictably vicious. While other sharks may avoid humans, the great white sharks are not so dependable in their actions. They have swum by wounded, bleeding people lying helplessly in the water and have savagely attacked other, perfectly sound individuals without warning. They can and will eat almost anything. Equipped with double rows of razor sharp, replaceable teeth—when one gets broken off another simply grows in its place—the shark will devour whatever it can fit in its mouth. Its stomach can stretch to several times its own size.

War, not sharks, was on George Kennaugh's mind as he was cruising on the troopship *Nova Scotia* during World War II. Kennaugh was working as a guard, watching over Italian soldiers who were prisoners of war bound for a prison camp in Europe. The ship was off the west coast of Africa one warm evening. Kennaugh had just gone off duty and had changed into a bathing suit to take a swim in the small pool aboard the ship. He was heading that way when a tremendous explosion shook the vessel. A German submarine had spotted the *Nova Scotia* and delivered a death blow to it with one torpedo.

In a matter of minutes the ship began to sink, so quickly Kennaugh didn't even have time to grab a life jacket. He dove off the ship and looking around he could see, scattered across the water's surface, hundreds of men clinging to life rafts and whatever debris would keep them afloat. Kennaugh himself found an oar drifting by and grabbed on to that. A short time later, a fellow crew member wearing a life jacket floated by and did the same.

The whole night the two men clung to the one oar hoping that somehow help would come soon. The next day passed with still no sign of rescue. That evening Kennaugh's shipmate had given up hope. He said he was just going to let go. He thought dying had to be better than clinging to one stick of wood with no prospects of help. But before he left he offered Kennaugh his life jacket.

As the man was loosening the straps, he suddenly let out a scream. His body rose straight in the air. A shark had swooped by and attacked. Then another and another and another came; they were drawn by the blood. Kennaugh swam away as fast as he could, but some of the sharks mistook him for the wounded man and began rushing at him. He splashed and kicked with all his strength and the sharks veered off. As he looked out over the water in the dim light of the stars he could see other men struggling and hear their screams all around him. There were sharks everywhere.

The water was swarming with ominous gray forms, sweeping out of nowhere and killing with a cruel, methodical precision. More and more, the night was filled with the horrible sounds of men shrieking and crying out as the sharks moved among them killing at random.

Gradually Kennaugh swam away from the center of all the killing and farther out to where a life raft was drifting. The men aboard it spotted him in the water and hauled him up onto it just as another group of sharks swam by. They continually circled the raft like underwater vultures moving in as close as they dared, nudging the raft with their snouts now and then. The men spent most of their waking hours clubbing the killers to drive them away.

This continued on into the next day when a Portuguese ship spotted them drifting and pulled in close to rescue the survivors. The sharks were still silently circling under them. There were so many and they were still so aggressive, the crew in the rescue boat had to beat them away with long, sharp boat hooks before they could bring the men to safety. Kennaugh and the men who shared that life raft with him turned out to be part of a very small and very lucky minority. After all the survivors were collected from the shipwreck, the final tally showed that out of nine hundred men, only one hundred ninety-two were left after this massive shark attack.

Not all the spectacular attacks happen way out at sea to stranded sailors. Skin diver Rodney Fox found this out as he was spear fishing in balmy Australian waters in 1963. He had his spear gun aimed at a fish when some enormous object came crashing into his side knocking the spear gun out of his hand. It only took a second to figure out it was a shark. Fox was then horrified to realize that the creature had also half-swallowed his left shoulder. Its jaws were clamped on his chest and back. He felt no pain, just shock and a kind of numb terror.

Fox tried to poke the shark in its eye and at the same time he clamped his legs around the shark's body, half-straddling the creature sideways as it streaked through the water. He was literally riding the shark like an underwater cowboy. In the struggle his mask was ripped off, Fox knew he couldn't last more than a few seconds without air. He had to breathe.

Finally the shark loosened its grip slightly and Fox broke for the surface of the water gasping for air. He looked around and saw a large cloud of blood, his blood, in the surrounding water. He also saw the deadly bulk of the great white shark swing around and bear down on him, its jaws wide open. Just as it swam by, Fox kicked hard, pushing it away for the moment.

It moved off, paused, and turned again heading in the general direction of Fox. It missed again, or so Fox thought. He had hung his bleeding catch from a small float that was attached to his belt by a thirty-foot cord. Smelling fish blood on the float, the shark had lunged for it, totally ignoring the man. But Fox wasn't safe. The creature had the float in its mouth and was diving, dragging Fox down with him. Fox was going deeper and deeper, faster and faster. Every second he was another few feet from the surface and air. Fox felt as though his lungs were going to explode. I'm going to drown, he thought. And he almost gave up. Then the line snapped and with what little strength he had left, Fox dragged his way back up the long distance to the surface of the water.

A patrol boat had seen the commotion and swung by to pick him up. What they found was a pale skin diver with a huge gash in his side. It was so painful, he could hardly breathe; but with the help of friends he managed to last long enough to get to the hospital and receive lifesaving attention.

Of course Fox was out in shark territory — the coast of Australia is infested with them — and way out in deep water. He was taking a greater than average risk of getting attacked by a shark, but not all that much greater. The truth is shark attacks can and do happen wherever there is ocean water.

In the summer of 1980 a young secretary named Phyllis Riley was riding piggyback on a friend's shoulders at a small beach in southern Delaware. They were in cool offshore water, not usually considered shark territory, and they were not in deep water. It was only four feet to the bottom.

Just the same, her friend had tripped and stumbled on what he thought was a jellyfish. Laughing, Phyllis fell into the water. When she stood up she saw what had tripped her friend. It was a shark. And it was heading right for her, its mouth open, its black eyes staring blankly. It swept by. And missed.

She began shouting "Shark!" and managed to get the attention of some of the people on the beach who were throwing Frisbees back and forth, or just lazing in the sun. A few people laughed. Some just stared. No one ran to help.

In the meantime the shark had circled around and come by again. It swept by and bit. It grabbed part of her bathing suit. With it clamped in its mouth, the shark turned and headed for the open sea. Phyllis saw the shoreline start to fade into the distance while she was being pulled away in the jaws of the creature. Fortunately for her, this didn't last long. The shark's teeth ripped the cloth. Part of her suit tore away, and she was free. The shark, not realizing he no longer had his kill, kept heading out to sea and disappeared. Experts said the last time anyone else ever reported a shark attack in those waters had been forty years before. It wasn't the kind of thing that was supposed to happen on a quiet summer beach in Delaware.

Even some of the gentler sea creatures can be infuriated into a killing state if men tamper with them too much. One example is the mammoth whale, the world's largest mammal. These creatures have been measured to be over one hundred feet long and to weigh more than one hundred eighty *tons*, roughly the size of a ship. In the 1800s the larger whales, such as the sperm whale, were hunted for the oil that could be made from their blubber, for their bones, and for a rare chemical called ambergris used in making fine, expensive perfumes. They were hunted by brave — some say foolish — men who chased the enormous mammals across the ocean in small boats and were armed only with harpoons.

When wounded, these enormous creatures were unpredictable and dangerous, as whale hunter James Bartley and his fellow whalers discovered on one hunt. Bartley was guiding the boat that was chasing a wounded whale. Before long, the situation was the other way around. The enormous mammal had dived, turned, and surfaced again heading straight for the small craft with the panicked whalers in it. It first rammed the boat and then caught it in its huge jaws. Most everyone managed to jump free, everyone but Bartley. After the whale had disappeared, there were stunned crewmen drifting among the pieces of the shattered boat. They were all rescued but when a head count was taken, Bartley was not among them. He apparently had been drowned or killed by the whale. One sailor said he thought he saw the whale swallow Bartley whole.

The ship cruised the waters looking for the whale. It may have died from its wounds and floated to the surface. Eventually sailors spotted a whale carcass drifting a short distance away. They slid over next to it, tied it to the side of the ship, and began cutting the blubber off it.

Judging by its looks and wounds, the whale resembled the one that had killed Bartley. To find out they decided to cut into the stomach and take a look and, if it was the whale that had swallowed Bartley, give his remains a decent burial at sea.

Little by little they sliced away the flesh and, to their amazement, the outline of a human body clearly appeared in the stomach. Working very carefully with their razor-sharp knives, they cut away the whale's stomach tissues and gradually freed the body of their swallowed crewman. The body was covered from head to toe with whale blood but perfectly preserved. Some men had expected that the powerful stomach acids of the whale might have dissolved all or at least some of his body. The men gently lowered the body of Bartley onto the deck.

Even more surprising is what followed. The supposedly dead man started coughing and gasping for air. The crew just stared for a few seconds before they realized what was happening. Then some of them took over giving Bartley artificial respiration while others massaged his limbs to restore circulation. He sat up and drank some brandy. Except for a splitting headache (and having an occasional bad dream in the years that followed) Bartley miraculously had few ailments from his time in the whale's insides. For a person who had been eaten whole, he was in amazingly good shape.

But not all the dangers of the sea are in the form of huge or vicious man-eaters. One of the stranger dealers of death in the ocean is a delicate creature called a sea snake. Somewhere back in the days of the dinosaurs one of these serpents' ancestors slithered from land into the sea and stayed there. Over the centuries these snakes made themselves quite comfortable. They developed a special tail to help them swim through the ocean. The tail has a long, vertical fin on it to push them along as they wiggle their bodies underwater. Like land snakes they breathe air, but they develop extremely large lungs so they can slip up to the surface of the water, take a deep breath of air, and swim for as long as two hours without another breath. Finally, like many of the land snakes, they are equipped with their own fangs and venom. Their poison is potent, so powerful that they are feared and avoided by just about every other creature in the ocean. Besides man they have only one other natural enemy, a bird called the sea eagle. When it sees a sea snake swimming near the surface of the water, the sea eagle swoops down, grabs the snake in its talons, and flies to shore where it drops the snake onto the rocks, killing it.

Fishermen, sailors, and skin divers in the warmer waters around the world head the other way when they spot a sea snake in the water. The reason is that they are so deadly. Although they are ordinarily not aggressive, sea snakes will bite if aggravated enough. And anyone who is bitten hard is certain to die. What helps prevent so many people from dying of sea-snake bites is the fact that their fangs are short and stubby and do not stick in deeply like a rattlesnake's. But people unlucky enough to be bitten by sea snakes seldom, if ever, live to talk about it. Their venom is ten times as deadly as a cobra's.

There is one story, for example, of a Chinese

fisherman who was emptying his net when he felt a small prick, the kind you would feel if you poked yourself with a pin. He thought nothing of it until he saw, to his horror, a sea snake wiggle out of the net. Minutes later his hand, and then his whole arm became swollen to almost twice their normal size. In spite of the frantic efforts of fellow fishermen to get him medical help, the man died minutes later.

Stories like this were in the back of the mind of researcher Kenneth MacLeish, who was studying and photographing sea snakes off the coast of Australia.

He knew better than anyone about the snakes' habits, and knew they would not bother him as long as he didn't try to capture one. Sea snakes are usually timid creatures that are usually slow to anger and attack. While diving underwater he spotted a pair of snakes gliding around each other in a slow, balletlike mating dance. He decided to move in for some pictures. As he got closer, one of the snakes quickly turned and swam straight for him, its mouth partly open in a striking position. Before MacLeish even had time to react, the fast-swimming reptile was right on top of him. It struck his arm once, twice, three times. MacLeish wheeled to move off and the snake struck again at his leg. And as a parting gesture, the furious animal lashed out one more time and bit into one of MacLeish's rubber fins. Then it turned away and dove for the deep.

When the attack was over, MacLeish carefully checked his body. Miraculously the snake's short fangs hadn't penetrated any part of the rubber wet suit he was wearing, but they had come close. He was literally a fraction of an inch — the thickness of his rubber suit — away from a quick but excruciating death.

In terms of deadly poison, nothing compares to a sea creature known as the stonefish. It's one of the most venomous fishes in the sea. As deadly fish go, it's not much to look at. It's an ugly lump of a fish only about a foot long. It weighs about two pounds at the most, and spends most of its life lying on the sea bottom looking exactly like a coral-covered rock or stone. It moves very little. It waits for a victim to come close enough to brush against one of many hollow needles that bristle from its back. As soon as that happens, poison shoots through the needle killing the victim in an instant. Its poison is so deadly that even one puncture from a single needle is more than enough to kill a full-grown man. Its venom is similar to a rattler's, only deadlier.

One of the few who was stung by a stonefish and lived was a fish expert named Dr. Joseph Smith. He was studying fish in the waters off the coast of East Africa and was well aware of the dangers of the stonefish's poison.

He had employed some natives to help with collecting fishes and one of them shouted that he had spotted a stonefish. Smith told him to save it for him. The people in that part of Africa all knew of the danger in picking up a stonefish. They had mastered a technique of scooping the fish off the sandy bottom without getting stung. They would deftly slip one hand under the stomach of the fish where there were no spines and then grab it tightly so it couldn't wiggle away. One man caught the stonefish this way, and put it in a tray to show to Smith later. So the fish would not die, he laid a cloth drenched with sea water over it.

Smith walked over to where the man was working and, not knowing what was in the tray, he reached in to put something there. His hand brushed against what he thought was just a wet rag. He felt a quick stab of pain and within ten seconds his thumb began throbbing. He asked the man what was under the cloth. The man pulled it back and showed the stonefish. Two of its spines were triggered in the poison release position.

Smith immediately began sucking the poison out of the small puncture wounds and wrapped a tourniquet around the thumb to keep the poison from spreading. He struggled up a steep path that led about a half mile to a lighthouse where some medicine was stored. As he walked he could feel the poison working with deadly speed. In minutes his hand was completely paralyzed and hot pains were shooting up his arm. By the time he reached the lighthouse the hand was swollen to almost twice its normal size and Smith was dizzy from the pain. His bad luck was not yet over. About to give him an injection of painkilling medicine, the lighthouse keeper slipped and dropped the glass bottle which shattered on the stone floor.

Fortunately Smith's wife arrived minutes later with more medicine. She was shocked at what she saw. Smith's arm was already beginning to swell up. He was vague and delirious and soaked with what she thought was water. It was perspiration pouring off his body. It actually made a puddle on the floor. The agonizing pain had moved up into his neck, shoulders, and back. Even standing was pure torture. More than once Smith felt he was going to pass out.

Soaking the arm in warm water seemed to ease the pain, and the swelling. With the help of much more medicine Smith managed to make it through the night. By morning his thumb was still swollen and almost completely black. If someone even brushed against his forearm he felt shooting pains move up and down it. Huge yellow blisters developed around the puncture wounds which oozed for a week.

After three days, some of the pain started to diminish and he could move his arm a little, but not without sharp aches and pains. His whole body was stiff and sore, and he needed heavy doses of penicillin to help the healing.

Even so, two weeks later his hand and thumb were still swollen and hard to move without pain, and the puncture wounds themselves did not really begin to get better until about a month and a half after he was stung. After he had healed, Smith found he could barely move his hand and thumb without feeling a lot of pain. He felt like this for three months.

When he first had seen the fish he measured it. He went and looked back in his records to see if his memory of how big it was, was correct. It was. The stonefish that almost killed him was just under four inches long. It weighed roughly three ounces.

Not all danger in the sea comes from a creature loaded with venom. What is considered one of the most dangerous and vicious of sea creatures, when provoked, is the moray eel. Over the centuries there have been many myths surrounding this fearsome creature: that it has venomous fangs; that most live in shipwrecks, sinuously weaving in and out of the skeletons of the dead crews who once manned the vessels; that if horsehairs were strewn on the ocean waters, each would turn into a moray eel.

The real facts are impressive enough. Resembling large, fat snakes, moray eels grow to seven or eight feet long. They nestle in crannies and nooks in coral reefs, for example, where they wait for unsuspecting fish to swim by and become their next meal. They somehow can also eat many of the poisonous creatures of the sea without being affected by the poison, although it has been suspected that it settles in their bodies. People who have caught and eaten moray eels have died from poison in the eels' flesh. The eels themselves have no fangs or poisons. Although they are not considered unusually aggressive, the moray eels can and do attack humans by using powerful jaws armed with needle-sharp teeth.

One Navy skin diver named Rudy Enders found this out the hard way, while diving off the coast of Florida one day. He was doing some spearfishing and after not seeing anything worth chasing, decided to call it a day. He was down in about thirty feet of water and was swimming up to the surface past an underwater ledge. Without warning, a green moray eel struck out, clamping its jaws on Enders's wrist. After a struggle, he managed to tear his arm free, but not without getting it torn up badly. His injuries and loss of blood were so bad, he had to spend several weeks in the hospital.

Months later, Enders had recovered and was spearfishing in the same area with a friend. As they were passing the exact same ledge where the attack took place, what looked like the same eel came rushing out of the same hole. Ignoring Enders's companion, it once more made a lunge straight at him, aiming this time not for the man's arm, but for his throat. He would have ripped Enders open if the other skin diver hadn't quickly raised his spear gun and fired. The spear hissed through the water and slammed into the side of the eel's head. Even that barely hurt the creature. The eel did swim off to one side, shook the spear free, and dove back into the maze of openings in the rocks. Enders started thinking about swimming someplace else.

One creature of the water world that prefers to stay closer to land and human prey is the saltwater crocodile. A distant relative of the American alligator, it is one member of that family of reptiles that has the most deserved reputation as a deadly man-killer. It is found mostly in the rivers and swamps of the Far East and in parts of Australia, and has established itself firmly in the animal kingdom as a feared killer. The best-known example of its savagery happened in the midst of a military battle.

During World War II, Japanese soldiers were retreating from the British on a small island off the coast of Burma where they had a particularly deadly meeting with these animals. Eighteen miles of swamp had separated the Japanese from the mainland. Rather than surrender they decided to try retreating through the swamp, fighting the British army every inch of the way. What they did not know at that time was that the swamp was also home to hordes of salt-water crocodiles. As the wounded Japanese soldiers fell, their blood trickled out into the water. This drew the blood-thirsty animals into the battle. They began stalking the Japanese soldiers.

That night the tide moved out of the saltwater swamp and left behind miles of mud and ooze that trapped both the wounded and the strong soldiers. And when the tide came back in, it brought the crocodiles. They moved in among the bogged-down men with a feeding frenzy, attacking anyone they could find. The night air was filled with the bloodcurdling screams of dying soldiers. Over one thousand men had retreated into the swamp that night. By morning, after the crocodiles had finished their killing, only twenty men were left alive.

This was the kind of creature a native aborigine named Mickey found himself facing as he and his friends traveled through one of the wilder parts of northern Australia. Mickey was in the lead when they came to a river. To cross it, he dove in and began swimming toward the other side. His friends followed. About halfway across something moved on the surface of the water and caught Mickey's eye. It was a salt-water crocodile raising his head.

Knowing it was too late to turn back, Mickey pointed out the crocodile to the others, and started to swim to shore underwater, hoping not to be spotted. As luck would have it, the current forced him downriver where the crocodile was resting, so as soon as Mickey broke the surface of the water there it was waiting for him.

Without wasting a second it attacked, clamping its powerful jaws on the man's legs. It started dragging the man underwater. Mickey beat and punched the animal, managing to poke his fingers into its eyes. The crocodile released him and Mickey, already weak from loss of blood, surged for shore once again. His friends were there waiting to help.

He had edged to within a few yards of the shore when the crocodile came back at him again, grabbing a leg and pulling him under. Then one of Mickey's friends jumped at the crocodile, shouting and splashing. The noise startled the animal enough to release the man. Mickey's friends grabbed him and pulled him away.

Both of Mickey's legs were badly lacerated. The main blood vessels were cut. It looked like he would soon bleed to death. Not giving up, his friend put mud on the cuts to stop the bleeding and threw Mickey over his shoulder. He set out to find help. For five days he carried Mickey, resting no more than a few minutes at a time. Eventually, he reached a small village with an airstrip. There they got on the radio, a plane flew in, took Mickey to a hospital, and against all odds, he survived.

Four

Death in the Skies

You would think that there is probably not a less friendly or forgiving place for a human to be than up in the air with the clouds and the birds. It is not like being in the water where, if your ship sinks, you can still swim, or being on the ground where you can step out of a car that breaks down. If you make one serious mistake thousands of feet in the air, there's no easy way out. You can't afford to slip up.

But there are times, a few times, when people have shown that with a little skill and a huge amount of luck, they have been able to overcome even the most deadly odds of surviving thousands of feet above the surface of the earth. They got a second chance.

For example, there's an old belief that anyone who falls from a great height will be dead before he hits the ground. The theory said that the speed with which a person falls creates such a wind that the tumbling person would no longer be able to breathe. For that reason it would only be a matter of seconds before his whole system broke down from lack of oxygen.

A British airman named Nicholas Alkemade disproved this theory by a spectacular accident. It happened during World War II when he was a crew member in a bomber cruising over Germany. Antiaircraft fire had zeroed in on his plane. Two shells made direct hits and in a matter of seconds flames were sweeping through the fuselage. Alkemade knew the plane was doomed to crash, or worse, maybe even explode in midair.

He had no intention of dying on a flaming aircraft eighteen thousand feet in the sky, so he decided to bail out. The only problem was he had no parachute. None was available in his part of the plane. He jumped anyway, reasoning that dying from the fall would be less painful than being burned to death. So, saying one last prayer, he leaped to his death. Or so he thought.

Gradually his falling body picked up speed until it was rocketing toward the ground at about one hundred twenty miles an hour. The ground was moving up at him at a fantastic rate. He closed his eyes and waited for the impact. A few seconds later he went smashing into the ground. Although he hadn't noticed it, Alkemade happened to jump over a heavily forested patch of land. The area was densely packed with pine trees of all sizes.

Moving at the high speed that he was, his body first went tearing through the upper parts of the trees like a cannonball ripping off branches. He bounced and tumbled from branch to lower branch. He finally crashed through the last, lowest branch and went thudding into a large snowbank.

Alkemade lay there stunned for a while not quite believing what had happened. He was alive. He stared up at the sky through the tunnel of shattered branches his body had made and blinked. He felt the cold snow melting on his face. He knew he was alive, but somehow couldn't quite accept it. He moved his arms. They were fine. His legs? They worked well too, although he felt a sharp pain in one foot. Later he was to discover he had sprained his ankle, his only serious injury aside from the bruises and scrapes from hitting the tree branches.

In time a German patrol, which had spotted his fall from the plane, came by expecting to bury the body of a British airman. Instead they found a scratched and slightly bruised Air Force sergeant limping through the snow. They took him prisoner. A few even looked around for a parachute, thinking that maybe they hadn't seen it open. They never found one. With some amazement they brought their lucky-to-be-alive prisoner in.

Of course, there were still skeptics who said that Alkemade hadn't fallen far enough to disprove that a human could not withstand a great fall. They said that if Alkemade had been at a higher altitude, he wouldn't have been able to breathe and eventually his heart would have given out from lack of oxygen. In 1960, Captain Joseph Kittinger proved this false by doing what no human had ever done before, or has done since, in a historic jump. After riding just a little over sixteen miles in a balloon straight up off the surface of the earth, he put on a parachute, double-checked his oxygen tank — the air was too thin to breathe — and jumped. He fell eighty-four thousand seven hundred feet, over sixteen miles. At times he was traveling at speeds of over six hundred miles per hour in the thin upper atmosphere before he finally decided to pull the ripcord on his parachute. That was, and is, the longest any human has fallen (and lived) before opening his parachute.

This doesn't mean, of course, that you can't get hurt going from sky to earth without a parachute. Every year a handful of people die in skydiving accidents where their parachutes never open or don't fully open. But even when that happens, some people still live. Maybe they aren't exactly ready to get up and dance after they've hit the ground, but they're alive.

In the fall of 1980, for example, one experienced parachutist named Ken Hamilton was going to give an unusual demonstration of his skills. He proposed to climb to the top of an eight hundred seventy-six-foot tall tower of the New River Gorge Bridge near Charleston, West Virginia, and, with a parachute on his back, dive off the tower, and float gently to the ground.

He made the climb, got set at the top of the tower, and dove out into thin air. When he felt he was far enough away from the bridge, he pulled his ripcord. But something went wrong. The parachute unfurled but didn't pop open as it was supposed to. Instead it half-dragged behind him like a streamer as he fell faster and faster toward the rocky shore. The crowd watched helplessly as

Hamilton's body slammed into a large boulder at the foot of the bridge. Police and ambulance ran over and were amazed to find him still breathing. He was rushed to a local hospital and when the doctors had finished looking him over they gave a damage report. The fall had broken his pelvis, shattered both his kneecaps, and smashed most of his teeth. Other than that, he was fine. Asked what his plans were when he got out of the hospital, Hamilton answered, "I'll probably jump again as soon as I'm physically able." And he added, "It's a relatively safe sport."

Jumping out of an airplane or even off the top of a bridge is not everyone's idea of a fun sport, much less a safe one. Even so, there are those who have done it, but not by choice, and certainly not for fun. One of the most famous unintended midair exits without a parachute happened during World War I to an American airman named Captain J. H. Hedley. He was sitting in the back seat of an old-fashioned, two-seater biplane piloted by a Canadian airman. The two men were flying at roughly fifteen thousand feet over the German line, when a small group of German planes zipped out of the clouds in attack formation.

To avoid the enemy aircraft the pilot suddenly nosed the plane over into a steep, screaming dive. It caught the Germans completely by surprise and he got away. Unfortunately it caught Hedley by surprise as well. The force of the sudden dive lifted him up from his seat and right out of the airplane. Out of the corner of his eye the pilot caught a glimpse of poor Hedley drifting off into the atmosphere. He figured the man was as good as gone and kept diving.

Eventually the pilot leveled off, and as he did he felt a sharp thump in the back of the plane. Taking a quick look around he spied Hedley hanging on to the tail for dear life. Apparently the steep dive created such strong air suction that Hedley was towed along by it and was able to grab on to the tail of the plane.

With the pilot holding the aircraft steady, Hedley was able to make his way over the tail and crawl along the fuselage of the plane until he got back to his seat. And when the two men finally reached their home base they had an interesting little story to tell their fellow pilots.

Of course, the airplanes made today don't have open cockpits and the pilots don't sit in an exposed seat. For that reason, this kind of thing isn't likely to happen anymore. Or is it?

In December of 1980 a civilian Army pilot named James Tobin and his copilot were making a routine delivery flight from New Jersey to Maryland in a small twin-engine plane. They had just taken off when Tobin noticed a small red warning light blink on his instrument panel. It showed that something was wrong with an exit door which had a built-in stairway. It wasn't shut tightly. Tobin's copilot took over the controls while he went back to see what was wrong. Tobin was wearing no parachute.

He had been gone for a couple of minutes when the copilot became suspicious that something was wrong. The warning light for the exit door was still on and Tobin had not returned. Glancing over his shoulder through the open cockpit doorway, the pilot could see the exit door wide open and no sign of Tobin. After setting the plane on automatic pilot he ran back to check. Looking out he saw the door had dropped completely open and down. Hanging off the edge, his legs just barely clinging to the stairway railing, was James Tobin, the pilot.

What the copilot didn't see was what had happened a minute or so before. Tobin had walked up the hatch to see what was the matter with it. Just as he did, the hatch, which was also a stairway, dropped from under his feet and opened out. In less than a second Tobin found himself lying on this small hatch nine thousand feet above the ground. Instinctively he grabbed the first thing that came to hand. It was the flimsy railing attached to the stairway. He had curled one arm around it and one of his legs as well.

Hanging on was not easy. Even at its cruising speed the plane was moving very fast, over two hundred miles an hour. The heavy wind resistance created by this speed was leaning on Tobin's body pushing him off the stairs, weakening his grip. He didn't know how long he could last on but later he remembered thinking, "If I want to live, I guess I'm going to have to hang on to this thing." His arm was killing him. He had hurt it when the hatchway fell out. He felt himself getting a little weaker.

In the meantime his copilot had quickly sized

up the situation and rushed back to the cockpit. He radioed for an airfield to give him clearance for an emergency landing. The nearest one was about forty miles away. After getting permission he set his course and headed straight for it.

When the people at the airfield looked up, they saw the small plane circling slowly with its side door open. Dangling over the edge of that door was the head of the pilot, James Tobin. As the plane came in to make its landing, Tobin realized he had another problem. His head was hanging over the bottom step which was supposed to touch the ground. If he stayed in that position, he would be dragged along the runway as the plane landed. Gradually the landing gear came down and the plane dipped toward the runway.

As the plane's landing gear touched down, Tobin tried to hold his head clear of the ground, which was blurring by underneath him. There was probably no more than ten or twelve inches' clearance between his face and the ground and that was only because he was forcing himself to hold his head up. The people watching the landing held their breath. They were certain the man's head was going to be pinned between the steps and the runway and crushed. Gradually the plane began to slow and finally stopped. Tobin relaxed his grip and lowered his head. His neck ached from the strain.

At the hospital doctors found out he had broken his shoulder in the fall and, except for being a little shaken up, was otherwise all right. Investigators who went out to look at the plane could not figure out what had happened, how the door had suddenly dropped open. Nothing appeared defective. Everything seemed to be working well. An accident like that just couldn't happen, but James Tobin knows it can and did, and almost cost him his life.

Equally hair-raising was the most spectacular of air crashes to happen to a single plane in a cold, still mysterious part of the world, the lofty Himalayas on the border between Tibet and China. During World War II, that stretch of mountains, which includes the world's highest peak, Mt. Everest, was known as "The Hump" by the pilots who risked their lives flying military supplies over the mountain range daily. Making that trip over and back required a powerful airplane, good piloting skills, and, very often, a lot of luck. Enemy pilots and antiaircraft guns waited on the China side for any supply planes brave enough or foolish enough to venture by. Even those who managed to escape enemy gunfire often were done in by the savage and unpredictable weather and the winds that prowled along the face of the mountains.

Captain C. J. Rosbert and his copilot Ridge Hammel had more than once survived air attacks from enemy planes. What they did not know was that on this one particular day they would have to survive a challenge from their other enemy, the mountains. Rosbert and Hammel and their radio operator were making one last flight that day into China with their heavily loaded plane. Clearing the mountains was always difficult when the plane was weighted down so heavily, but today it seemed particularly bad.

There was heavy rain, which turned to snow as they climbed higher. They could barely see beyond the nose of the plane as they moved along at their cruising speed of one hundred eighty miles an hour. But they were no more concerned than usual. They knew that by climbing just a thousand more feet they would be out of the bad weather and up over the top of the mountain.

But they just couldn't gain that thousand feet. Ice started to form on the wings, first thinly, then heavily. In a few minutes it was close to six inches thick. Not only was the plane not able to climb anymore, it had started dropping, slowly and steadily. They were gradually nosediving down, toward the mountains.

To make matters worse, ice began to cake over the windshield. Soon it was completely blocked out. Captain Rosbert laid his bare hand against the glass to melt a viewing hole in the ice. When his hand got numb he laid his other one against it. Gradually he made what amounted to a peephole in the icy windshield a fraction of an inch in diameter. When he peeked through it, all he could see at first was the smoky haze of a cloud. When the cloud thinned out, he could see the top of a mountain straight ahead. Grabbing the controls, he pulled away hard.

He knew he had barely missed the peak and was about to breathe easily when another dark shape suddenly loomed up. Then there was a jolt and a sickening tearing noise at the bottom of the plane's cabin. The men were slammed around. Rosbert felt a terrible pain shoot up his left leg. The engines roared briefly, then stopped.

There was total silence. Looking through the windshield he could see snow falling. He knew what had happened but he couldn't believe it. They had flown straight into the side of a mountain, at 180 miles per hour. The altimeter on the plane's instrument panel showed they were sixteen thousand feet above sea level.

Rosbert looked around. The radio operator was dead. His copilot had been thrown against one side of the plane. Blood was running down his face, which was so battered that one eye was already swollen shut. But he was alive. Hammel had trouble moving around. His left ankle was swollen and painful.

Neither man could move very well because of his injuries. Just struggling to get the emergency rations out of the storage boxes took most of the day. By the time they had gathered up the food and a couple of parachutes to use as crude sleeping bags, they were exhausted and fell into a troubled sleep.

The next morning they had their first chance to find out where they were. As it turned out Captain Rosbert, by pure dumb luck, had banked the plane so that it lined up with the slope of the mountain face and did a belly flop of a landing. Had he tilted the wings just a little more or managed to fly a little farther, he would have smashed the plane head-on into a wall of stone, a mountain peak just fifty feet ahead of where they finally did land. Had they hit at the speed they were flying it would have meant certain death for all of them.

All they really knew was that they were sixteen thousand feet up somewhere in the Himalayan mountains, but where was a total mystery. From where they were standing they could see no sign of civilization or any sight of a rescue plane. Even if one flew by, it would never spot them. The plane was buried under three feet of snow. Their only hope of staying alive was to get off that mountain and somehow find help. They checked their food supply. There was enough to keep them alive for about six days. After that they were on their own.

After picking out a route down the mountain they decided to wait five days to rest their injured ankles; but by the third day they were too anxious. They had to get out. They set out at dawn. They gathered up their food and headed down to the timber line, where the forest began. They knew they had to make it before sundown or they would freeze to death, completely exposed on the face of the mountain all night. It was at least a mile down to the timber line. Struggling and stumbling painfully on their injured feet through the snow they crawled along using all their strength. By the time half the day had gone they looked back to check their progress. They were barely two hundred yards from the plane. At that rate they wouldn't even be close to the forest by sunset.

To avoid being stranded out on the bare snow field at night they groped their way back up to the plane and tried to figure out what to do next. By then they only had one day's supply of food between them. They had to think of something soon.

And they did. During the night they ripped boards up off the floor of the plane and built a crude sled. When morning came they strapped themselves and their supplies on their homemade toboggan and took off. They covered the first one hundred yards in about thirty seconds. When the sled got bogged down in the snow, they tried a different technique. They held their feet, lay on their backs, and went slipping and flipping down the snowy slope on their backs like a pair of overturned turtles. The tumbling eventually brought them to the edge of the bare mountain face. The next part was a five-hundred-foot slope, so steep it was almost a sheer drop. They had no way of knowing if they could make it down alive.

Since his leg was in better shape, Hammel went first, dropping over the edge with a whoop. He disappeared in a cloud of snow. There was a scream, a long silence, and then his voice saying, "Come down. It's rough, but it's okay." Rosbert threw himself down and for what seemed like hours he was sliding and skidding blindly through the snow. He hit the ground at the bottom so hard that for an instant he thought he had broken his back.

That long slide led them to a river which they followed as best they could over the rough, mountainous terrain. They managed to skimp on their one day's food supply so that it lasted a full eight days. In more than a week of trudging they reached what looked like a dead end — the river dropped off into a long waterfall and they were trapped between the sheer rock walls of a narrow canyon. They were out of food, far from any access to the river, and, it seemed, out of luck.

At that moment Hammel spotted a sturdy-looking vine. With it they managed to climb up and out of the small canyon to what turned out to be a cleared trail, one marked out by people. For three days, without a scrap of food in their stomachs, they followed the trail, almost faint with the lack of food.

Five days later they reached a fork in the river and had to make a decision about which way to go. Their lives hung in the balance. The wrong turn could set them off on a path of endless wandering until they starved to death in some bleak, forsaken area in the foothills of the Himalayas. Taking a wild guess, they went to the right.

A few miles later they found the remains of a recently abandoned village. Moving on after a brief rest they came across another village inhabited by a strange group of primitive-looking people. These, they later learned, were the Mishmi, a tribe of almost prehistoric natives who wandered the hills of Tibet living much the way humans had done in the Stone Age. They wore very little clothing, just a scrap of leather around their waists and no shoes or sandals. They were armed only with crude handmade knives.

They were simple, friendly people who took in the two injured pilots, fed them, gave them shelter, and studied with amazement their pale skin and peculiar clothing. They never seemed to tire of listening to the ticking of the airmen's watches, turning their flashlight off and on, and working the zippers on their leather flight jackets.

Rosbert and Hammel stayed with these tribes people for a few weeks, gradually regaining their strength and trying to figure out how to get word out to civilization that they were still alive. An opportunity came when an itinerant trader wandered into the village. He wanted them to follow him, but their injuries still hadn't healed enough to let them. The next day he sent his son to stay with them. Both father and son had seemed fascinated by the pencil the two men had. The airmen decided to stay on their good side, and they wrote a short note to the father. It said they were two American fliers who had crashed in the mountains and that they would visit him when their wounds had healed. The young man solemnly took the penciled note and disappeared. The pilots needed the father's contact with the outside world, and they hoped that note would keep him happy.

Four days later the son reappeared from the wilds of Tibet and handed them, neatly folded in a wax-sealed envelope, a telegram. It was from a British officer who happened to be leading a scouting party a short distance away when the young man came upon them. He handed them the penciled note written by the two Americans.

Two days later a British army doctor walked into their primitive village and looked the two American airmen over. He told them that they were the first white men ever to appear in that part of the world. What is more, the odds of any friendly army force being in the general vicinity of where they had ended up were minuscule, since no army contingent had ever been in that part of the world. "It was one chance in a million, and we had hit it," said Captain Rosbert.

The doctor examined them, patched up their cuts and bruises, and told Rosbert he had a broken ankle. But they had been lost so long that the broken ankle had healed itself.

After two weeks of rugged hiking they managed to make it out of the mountains back to the British camp and eventually to their own base. The pilot, Captain Rosbert, was flown back to the United States where his healed but crooked ankle was repaired. The copilot, Ridge Hammel, went back to his air base and got ready to fly "The Hump" all over again.

Five

They Walked Away from Death

There are those among us who have seen death come and go without ever being touched by it. They seem to lead charmed lives, sidestepping certain catastrophes almost without thinking. They are the people who, when disaster strikes, are still standing when everyone around them is laid low. It's a talent you can't learn, a skill you cannot acquire. Either you are born to be the victim of disaster or, like Ray Linnen, you are born to be a survivor.

Linnen first realized he had this knack of avoiding certain death when he was eight years old. He was standing on a street corner in Arkansas City, Kansas, and was about to cross the street when some unknown urge made him step back onto the curb and wait a few seconds. He had barely made it when a car came roaring by out of nowhere, sideswiped a pedestrian, and smashed into a telephone pole. As a result of the accident three people died, but young Ray Linnen was not one of them.

Later in his life he got a job at the Golden Rule Refinery near Wichita. He was working the late shift at the refinery, going around checking the equipment periodically to make sure that everything was always in operating order. Just before his last machinery inspection his replacement came to work a little earlier than usual. Linnen was going to stay but the man insisted he take off a little early and go home. Since what the man said made sense, Linnen took his advice and left. His replacement headed out to make an inspection tour of the machinery, the one Linnen would ordinarily have made. Minutes later a faulty boiler exploded. The other man died in the blast.

A few years later he was working in another part of Kansas manning an oil rig. It was hot and dusty, and the work was tiring. He had gotten into the habit of stopping by a small ice-cream parlor in a nearby town, Udall, to take an ice cream break before heading home. He did it every night, automatically.

Then one night as he was heading home he was feeling a little more tired than usual and somehow didn't have his daily yearning for an ice-cream cone. When he came to the tiny town of Udall, he drove straight through instead of stopping. Five minutes later what was to become known as the deadliest tornado in the history of Kansas was swirling its way across the plains. It touched down in Udall and left behind it a trail of death. Of the town's four hundred fifty people, two hundred were injured and seventy-three were killed by the tornado. Seven of those dead had been sitting in the town's ice-cream parlor at the moment the tornado hit. It leveled the small building. At that moment Linnen was not in his usual seat in the parlor but miles down the road, very much alive.

When asked why he always happened to be one step ahead of death, Linnen offered, "There's a time and a place for everybody's death. It just hasn't been my time yet."

The charmed life can begin much earlier for other people. It did for Brian Karnbach, who was only a month and a half old at the time of his brush with death. It was a hot summer day and he was riding with his parents back to their home in a small town in New York State. On the way home the parents pulled the car over to the side of the road to take a brief rest. They took out young Brian and put him, still sitting in his infant car seat, on the roof of the car.

In their confusion and rush to continue on their way, the adults completely forgot about the baby sitting quietly on top of the car. They started the car up again and headed on down the road still forgetting about the small baby riding alone on the car roof. They went a couple of miles and the baby stayed quietly in his seat watching the scenery flash by. After one bump too many the seat and the baby in it slipped and fell.

The parents in the meantime were all caught up in talking about what they had done that day and were driving along totally unaware of who was missing. It wasn't long before they realized, first of all, that their baby was gone, and secondly, that they had left him on top of the car. Coasting slowly to a stop they pulled over to the side of the road and nervously looked on top. There was no baby there. They frantically climbed back into the car and retraced their route cruising slowly down the road looking for some sign of the baby and the seat. After hours of searching they found nothing. "We were hysterical," the mother said.

What they had no way of knowing was that little Brian had toppled off the car roof and lay there in the middle of a busy highway miraculously untouched by traffic. Finally, a driver going by took the time for a good look. What he thought was just a package that had fallen off a car or truck was a small seat with a little person strapped in it. He pulled over to the side of the road and, risking his life in the traffic, hopped out into the busy road, scooped the baby off the ground, and brought him back to his car. He drove a short distance down the road until he found a hospital. He left the baby there. When the doctors looked over the screaming child they were amazed to find that except for a mild sunburn, the child was unharmed. In the meantime his parents, frantic with worry, had gone to the police, and with their help managed to trace their son. They were finally reunited with what one newspaper called their "miracle tot."

What is probably a more famous escape from death on the roads, for some, involved a famous movie actor, a cursed car, a master auto mechanic, and a college student. The actor was James Dean who, in the 1950s, had become famous as a rebellious, romantic actor on the screen and a racing car driver off the screen. Once he became famous he soon became wealthy and liked to spend his spare time and money driving expensive sports cars in and around Hollywood. He drove so wildly and so fast that the directors and movie companies for whom he worked often made him give up driving while he was working on a movie to make sure he would live long enough to finish it.

He never lost his interest in racing, and as his paychecks got bigger so did the price tags on the cars he bought. The last one he was to buy was the fastest and one of the most expensive sports models of his day. It was a sleek, silvery car called the Porsche Spyder. It could do well over one hundred fifty miles an hour without straining.

Dean bought the car under one condition: that the company's master mechanic go with the car to races and work on it personally. The man chosen for this was a young but brilliant Porsche mechanic named Rolf Wuetherich, who was considered one of the best in California.

Oddly, there were those who had worked on Dean's car and had ridden in it who said it gave them a "bad feeling," according to author Richard Winer in his book *Haunted Houses*. For example, one relative warned Dean to be careful in the car, that he was "sitting on a bomb" and should drive with caution. Dean just laughed when he heard this and sped off defiantly.

In October of 1955 he had entered the car in a big race in Salinas, California. Usually his crew took the expensive car to the race location in a specially built trailer, but this time Dean wanted to drive there himself. His faithful mechanic, Wuetherich, climbed into the car with him and together they spun down the highway with the road crew following and towing the empty trailer. Just about the time Dean left, another young man, a total stranger named Donald Turnipseed, had left for home heading in the opposite direction. Unlike Dean he drove a slower, older car. Getting home, not racing, was on his mind.

Gradually, unknowingly, the two drivers moved toward each other over the network of California roads, Dean heading north speeding along at what was later estimated to be eighty-five miles an hour and Turnipseed doing the more cautious speed limit. Any number of things could have kept the two from ever seeing each other on the road, but that afternoon something seemed to be working so that the paths of their two cars would cross at one very deadly spot. No one, not Turnipseed, nor James Dean, nor Rolf Wuetherich, had any way of knowing it, but in a matter of minutes each of them would be face to face with death. Only one of them would succumb.

Dean drove fast but well, streaking down the road, pausing once to pull over at a roadside restaurant to eat and let his road crew catch up. Of course, no one can tell how much of a difference that stop made in his date with death; if he had stayed longer or hadn't stopped at all it might have kept him from being in the wrong place at the wrong time.

In any case Dean and Wuetherich climbed back into the car and again went speeding down the highway. There was no one in sight and Dean held the car to well over eighty miles per hour. The sun had settled a little lower and the blood-red glare flashed in Dean's eyes. He was on a long straightaway and wasn't worried much about being surprised by any traffic. Wuetherich was getting chilly in the speeding car with its top down, and began to reach into the back seat for a jacket. A few miles down the road Turnipseed began slowing down to get ready to make a left turn. If he had bothered to listen, he would probably have heard the roar of a powerful sports car coming at him from the opposite direction. But he didn't. Slowly he began to turn. Wuetherich heard Dean scream something and looked up from where he was getting the jacket. Up ahead an old car was making a left turn across their lane. It was still dozens of yards away, but at the speed Dean's car was traveling those yards disappeared fast.

At the same instant Donald Turnipseed saw this silver car coming at him with what seemed like the speed of a bullet. He followed his instincts and slammed on his brakes. As a result he was sitting in the middle of the lane as the car carrying James Dean and his mechanic came slamming into him.

There was a huge noise and then the impact was a blur to all three men. When all was quiet Turnipseed lay across the front seat of his car. There was blood running down his face. Rolf Wuetherich's body had been thrown about twenty-five feet from where the Porsche finally stopped. And the driver of that car was still behind the wheel.

When the wreckage was cleared the ambulances arrived, and the three men were rushed to a nearby hospital. James Dean, it turned out, had died instantly on impact. The force of the crash broke his neck. Rolf Wuetherich was still half-conscious when the ambulance attendants found him. He, it turned out, had a broken leg and a broken jaw, and would spend weeks in the hospital to recuperate. Turnipseed was treated for a bloody nose and some cuts on his face and walked out of the hospital the same day.

Some say the tragic story of James Dean's car didn't end there. Other people who used salvageable parts of the car or even came too close to it had bad luck. A doctor who bought the engine died in a racing accident and another driver, who had the transmission from the Spyder installed in his car, was crippled in a crash. Another man who bought two usable racing tires from the car barely missed having a deadly accident himself when both tires mysteriously blew out at the same instant. A truck driver who had been transporting the wrecked car to another town lost control of the truck and was thrown out of the cab. Dean's death car broke loose from the back of the truck and fell on the driver, killing him.

Of course, many people have made fun of the cursed-car theory and point out, correctly, that there is no way to prove it. Just the same, it did seem to bring death to a very select group, those who didn't have the skill or luck to escape the curse that hung over the car. Only a few lucky ones beat the curse.

What can be just as mysterious is why some people are spared and others are not when disaster strikes either on a small scale, like a crash, or on a large one, like a flood. In 1972, an Eastern Airlines plane, known to the aircraft controllers as Flight 401, was getting ready to land in a Florida airport one night when it suddenly and mysteriously crashed in the Florida Everglades. As a result one hundred and one passengers and crew were killed and the plane was destroyed. But amazingly, seventy-seven people survived.

As nearly as crash investigators were able to figure it out, the trouble began when one of the landing gears didn't seem to be set right for the plane's landing. The only way to tell for sure, it turned out, was to climb down into the cubbyhole where the landing gear was and take a look. One of the crew members, Second Officer Repo, had climbed down to do just that.

While this was going on, no one seemed to have noticed that the plane was losing altitude, that it was slowly drifting down below the safe two thousand-foot level. The plane did have a built-in safety device, a soft warning chime to tell the crew that they were going off course. The problem was that this chime only sounded in one part of the cockpit, at the console where Second Officer Repo sat. Unfortunately he was not there when it went off and no one else heard it.

As a result the plane was slipping steadily closer and closer to the ground without the crew ever realizing what was happening. By the time they did, the plane was only a few hundred feet over the desolate Florida Everglades and seconds from total destruction.

Once the plane had dipped too low, an edge of its left wing got snagged in the ground and the rest of the airplane slammed into the ground, plowing a trough through the swamp. When the plane hit it was shattered into a thousand pieces. The passengers were flung around like so many rag dolls; some, still strapped in their seats, landed yards away from where the plane hit, while others remained part of the speeding crumbling aircraft until it finally snapped apart. The eeriest thing about the crash was what one might call the pattern of death.

Very often when a plane crashes and there are survivors, those who die are concentrated in one part of the plane, and those who live are in another part. In this crash there was no such pattern. In one row of the plane all six people survived while everyone sitting right in front of them didn't. Even stranger was how in another row one man survived while the person sitting next to him died. By the airlines' safety board judgments, this was not the kind of crash that anyone was supposed to have survived because the plane was totally destroyed. But contrary to the rules, people did.

Among the survivors were Barry Connell and his wife, Ann. They had originally planned to take another flight but ended up not taking it. Instead, as luck would have it, they were scheduled to fly on Flight 401.

Even though they were on a doomed airplane, luck turned in their favor. They were offered seats in the first class section but they decided against taking them. They preferred instead to sit in tourist class. That turned out to be a life-saving decision. As it happened, most of the people who were sitting in first class did not survive.

Just before the crash Connell was quietly reading a book when he felt the left side of the plane jolt suddenly. That was followed immediately by a crazy, twisting ride along the ground when the rest of the airplane hit. Instinctively he reached out to protect his wife and pulled her toward him as they rode out the crash and heard the horrible noises that were the sounds of the metal fuselage being ripped to ribbons.

By the time they came to a stop, the top of the plane where they were sitting had been torn off as though it were made of paper. The floor was tilted crazily to one side and Connell was dangling out of his seat by his seatbelt. He managed to unfasten his belt and drop down to where his wife was. Miraculously, neither was badly hurt. The force of the crash had literally blown their part of the plane wide open, but left them untouched. Their biggest problem was where to go to wait for help. As they struggled through the icy swamp waters in the pitch-black night, a powerful smell arose. It smelled like some kind of gasoline. Connell quickly figured out it was jet fuel from the plane. Impact probably tore the tanks open and spilled it all around the crash area. As it turned out many of the passengers were covered with the explosive fuel on impact.

Together Connell and his wife sought out one of the few pieces of the plane. There they huddled above the swamp waters and waited for their rescuers, who were to come hours later. On another pile of debris another group of survivors had clustered together.

One of these was a car transmission dealer

named Al Morris who had a similar run of bad and good luck. He originally had been scheduled to take off on another flight but decided to switch to Flight 401 at the last minute because the time was so convenient. It was a change of schedule that could have cost him his life.

But it didn't. He first realized how serious the crash was when he looked up and saw, to his amazement, the front of the plane start to fold up in his direction. The instant the plane stopped moving he quickly looked around for the nearest way out. The only available exit was a hole ripped in the side of the plane. Morris dragged himself out and he helped other passengers squeeze through the painfully narrow opening and scramble onto a pile of debris above the swamp water. There they banded together shouting simultaneously for help. His sides ached fiercely and breathing was painful. When he was later taken to the hospital he soon found out the reason: his rib cage had been crushed by the impact of the crash.

While this was going on, a hunter named Bob Marquis was cruising that part of the Everglades. He happened to see the plane go down. He was one of the first on the scene to pull survivors out of the water into his small flat-bottomed boat. Soon Coast Guard and military helicopters were in the area groping through the starless black night picking their way through the debris-strewn swamp, looking to rescue any survivors. To the amazement of many of those who came that night, not only were there survivors but many of them, like the Connells, were standing and waiting almost untouched. Investigators later were able to solve the mystery of the crash but not how anyone could have ever survived.

Few people were expected to survive and in fact few did survive a disaster of a different kind on May 31, 1889, in the small town of Johnstown, Pennsylvania. The town became internationally famous for one of the world's deadliest floods. A nearby dam built across a branch of the Conemaugh River formed a three-mile body of water known as Lake Conemaugh. As heavy rains fell, Lake Conemaugh got bigger and the dam that held it back, weaker. After days of this kind of weather, the inevitable happened. The dam split open and a wall of water roared down the river valley straight for Johnstown, washing most of it away.

Among the first to see the flood waters hit was a teenage boy named Victor Heiser. He was working in the general store his father, George Heiser, owned. They were doing a booming business that May morning, but by afternoon it had tapered off. The rain turned main street into a shallow pond, covered with two feet of water. People rushed home. As the waters rose higher, George Heiser began to get worried about the horses in his barn. If they began panicking when the water started to rise they could strangle on their tethers. He sent Victor out to the barn to untie them.

After taking off his shoes, Victor waded his way across the backyard to the barn, where he freed the horses. He had just stepped back outside the barn door when he heard what sounded like an enormous roar or explosion. Confused and terrified, he frantically looked around to see where it was coming from. He could see nothing, but one thing he knew for certain, whatever it was, was getting closer. He got ready to run for the house. As he did, he looked up and saw his father in a second story window waving him back to the barn.

Victor spun on his heels and ran for the barn and scuttled up a ladder to the roof. A trapdoor opened out onto it. He scrambled onto the sloping tin roof and gazed in the direction of the roar. He wasn't prepared for what he saw.

An enormous wall of water was sweeping through town pushing in front of it all the debris it had washed up in its path. All Victor could see at first was a gigantic wall of rubbish—rooftops, crushed walls, whole trees—rolling in his direction. It was like some gigantic living thing on a mad rampage. He watched it helplessly as it swallowed up one building after another in the town. All he could do was sit in the chilling rain and wait for it to reach him.

In seconds it seemed the waters moved down his street, engulfed his neighbor's house, crushing his own house as though it were paper, and, seconds later, the giant wave hit the barn. Instead of crushing it, the wall of water sent it rolling slowly, end over end, and young Heiser had to keep scrambling across the surface of it to stay on top, as though he were trapped on some mammoth rolling log. One slip and he was dead.

Fortunately another house came drifting by at this time and as it brushed against the barn he jumped onto the roof. That was only safe for a matter of seconds because it collapsed beneath him and began to be sucked into the huge wall of water and debris. Then another house slid by and he jumped for that, barely grabbing the eaves with his two hands. His grip wasn't firm. He knew he would be able to hang on only a short time and there was nothing left in sight to jump to. Beneath him a sea of jagged boards, broken glass, and tree branches waited to snag him and drag him under. He couldn't hold on any longer. He let go and dropped into the mass of debris.

Amazingly his luck still held. He landed on a large flat piece of wood which had just floated by. It was the roof of his barn on which he had been standing just minutes before. Clutching the scrap of roof, he rode it as though it were a raft floating on the wave, by now choked with the pieces of his shattered town.

While he lay on his crude raft a whole family, neighbors of his, went sliding by him on what was left of a floor of some building. As the man, his wife, and two children sat there helpless, a huge mass of debris—immense wooden beams, whole pieces of buildings—came slamming down on the group and crushed them. Minutes later Victor himself had a similar confrontation with death. A solid brick building up ahead had blocked the flow of shattered homes and other buildings. As a result, more and more flood debris was backing up around it. Each new wave would smash more into the jagged pile of glass and wood. Victor found himself riding on one of these waves.

His small piece of roof got caught against the side of the brick building and, for what seemed like years, he scrambled back and forth, dodging the heavy beams and the shattered trees that kept slamming into the spot where he was stuck. In the middle of all this an enormous shadow rose over the place where he was caught. He looked up, and at first thought it was an entire building. A second later he saw it was a freight car tilted up on end and about to topple exactly where he was. He tried to shake his raft loose, but it was stuck. The enormous freight car started to fall over.

At that second the brick building which had been causing this deadly blockage suddenly crumbled under the strain, creating a surge that neatly drew Heiser out from under the falling boxcar and shot him out to a clear spot in the floodstream.

The stream had carried him away from what he thought would be a safe area where he could jump free of his raft to a more open, dangerous section. This last time, however, his luck held. He coasted by another brick building where there was a group of other survivors huddled on its rooftop. When his bit of raft sailed by, Heiser grabbed the building and scrambled up to join them. Then they all sat there waiting patiently for the rescue boats to come and get them as they watched the remains of their town and their lives drift by.

Six

Survival

British explorer Sir Ernest Shackleton had those two things that always come through when someone is face to face with what seems like certain death: courage and luck, a lot of luck. He put a real strain on both when, in 1916, he found himself stranded during an expedition he had organized to explore the Antarctic. It was and, for that matter, still is one of the more mysterious parts of the world, and for any explorer one of the most dangerous.

Shackleton soon found this out when, after struggling through close to two thousand miles of half-frozen ocean waters, he saw his expedition stopped dead in its tracks. His wooden ship got caught in the treacherous icebergs in the Antarctic ocean and was eventually crushed under thousands of tons of pressure of moving ice. After five months of trying to work the ship free, Shackleton and the ship's crew were left with only one choice: let the ship die and save themselves. The twenty-eight men in the expedition squeezed themselves onto the three small lifeboats they had brought with them and set off for the nearest part of civilization, a dreary little spot on the map called Elephant Island, off the tip of South America.

Even that turned out to be impossible to reach. The weather, which was never good, became meaner. Fierce biting winds turned against them. For every mile of progress they made, they were pushed back three more. Totally exhausted and desperately low on food, they decided to give up and stop at the nearest island to remap their strategy.

The place they picked, an unexplored island, offered them nothing in the way of comforts. There was no food to be found there. There was only more of the monotonous landscape of ice and snow, and that gave them no protection from the subzero winds that ripped their tents to shreds, leaving them constantly exposed to the dangers of freezing to death.

Time was running out for the expedition crew. Without their ship, with very little food left, they could not last much longer. Finally Sir Ernest planned what they all knew was their last hope. With five of their best men, the best boat, and a small supply of food, he thought he might be able to make it to a small island called South Georgia and get help. It did not look like an easy trip. Somehow the men had to cover over eight hundred miles of the coldest and most treacherous ocean waters in the world and do it in a rowboat only twenty-two feet long. Of course, they had other choices. They could die by starvation or by freezing.

They launched the boat and for two weeks

struggled through an icy, unforgiving sea that constantly threatened to drown them. Wave after wave steadily swept over the boat. There was no dry place to stand or sleep. Each man had to take turns napping in subzero weather under a soaking wet sheet of canvas spread over the deck. The men got weaker and sicker from the strain. The weather was so consistently rough that whenever a man stood up to use his sextant and compass and plot the position of the boat, two other crewmen had to hold his legs so he would not get swept overboard. When the men began running out of hope, and food, they sighted the island of South Georgia.

But their troubles were not over. They tried to maneuver around to the other side of the island where there was a whaling station, but the swift currents and some more bad weather forced them back up on a desolate beach. The men had no choice. They would have to leave the boat behind and hike across miles of snow, ice, and mountains to the other side. Not everyone went. Three of the men were too sick and weak to walk one more step, so Shackleton and two others had to go the last few miles by themselves. They roped themselves together and started hiking up over the mountains toward the other side of the island. Fog and heavy mists slowed them down and at times almost caused their death. Once they had barely missed stepping off a two hundred-foot cliff in the fog. Another time they were trapped on the top of a mountain just as night started to fall. The way ahead was blocked by more fog and it was too late to turn back. Still, they had to get to a lower level or they would quickly die of exposure up on the icy mountain peak.

Slowly and painfully they groped their way down hacking a foothold, one step at a time, into the ice as they went. It wasn't long before they realized that tactic was hopeless. It would never get them off the mountain in time.

It was then that they decided to take a gamble. They rolled the long rope they carried into a wide, flat coil until it looked like a crude rug or pad. They slid it over to the edge of a ridge and the three men sat on it, one behind the other, as though they were riding a toboggan. They could see nothing down below them because of the fog, and the ridge was so steep it really looked more like a cliff. After taking one long breath, they pushed off.

For a few hair-raising seconds, they felt absolutely nothing underneath them. They were falling through thin air. At that instant they were convinced they had not pushed off on a ridge but off a sheer cliff, and that they were falling to certain death. That fear passed when they hit solid ground and started sledding down the steep slope. But a new one replaced it. It was so dark and foggy they could see nothing ahead of them. They were speeding down this hill totally in the dark. All they had to do was hit one large rock or hunk of ice and they were done for.

Luck was with them. Gradually their rope sled slowed and they glided to a stop at the bottom of the ridge. They struggled on and about half a day later the three men stumbled into the whaling station. Although Shackleton and his men were all known to those who worked at the station, no one recognized them. Shackleton's hair had turned completely white from the ordeal and he and his men were gaunt, ragged shadows of themselves. Once the shock of being safe wore off, Shackleton and his men got a boat and went back to rescue the rest of the expedition.

Not every story of survival is as inspiring. There are those who never bother to wait for luck to favor them and who stay alive at the cost of others' lives. One of the stranger stories of survival has to do with a western prospector by the name of Alferd Packer. He made his name as a survivor in a most bizarre way.

His story began in February of 1874 when he left the Colorado town of Montrose to guide five inexperienced miners to the gold fields in Breckenridge, in another part of the state. They left in the dead of winter, when most of the smarter, more experienced travelers preferred to stay home and wait for the snows to stop.

The group never reached Breckenridge and they were given up for dead. There was no word of any of them until April of that same year when Alferd Packer came stumbling out of the woods all by himself. His party got stranded in a blinding blizzard during which the pack mules carrying all their food and supplies panicked and ran off into the wilds leaving them stranded with what little food they had already unloaded. As the weeks wore on, the men died off one by one, of starvation or the cold, until the only one left was that savvy old prospector, Packer himself. He alone walked out of the mountains alive, weeks later. He said he lived off moss and melted snow until he was able to find his way back to civilization and safety.

His story seemed plausible except for one odd thing. Packer looked amazingly well fed for someone who had spent months in the wilderness living off next to nothing in the way of food. A close check of the site where Packer said he and his companions tried to weather out the blizzard did turn up the bodies of the five men. Closer examination showed they did not die of starvation but of gunshots. Worse than that, there was evidence that something, or someone, had attacked them, and eaten parts of them.

After a long conversation with the sheriff, Packer finally admitted his original story was false. He said one of the miners shot the other four and, to save himself, Packer shot the killer himself, which accounted for all the bullet-riddled bodies. Left with no supplies and little prospect of finding any more, Packer, in his hunger, ultimately ate some of his companions.

Packer was put on trial and convicted of cannibalism, the first person in the United States to be found guilty of that crime. At the time he passed sentence the judge was so upset he hollered out, "Dang you, Alferd Packer! There were only six Democrats in all of Hinsdale County and you had to go and eat five of them!"

Packer served his time and lived quietly in a suburb of Denver until a ripe old age. But his story and his unusual crime have not been forgotten. Students at the University of Colorado named their local eating place after him. It's called the Alferd Packer Memorial Grill and once a year they celebrate Alferd Packer Day. To honor the memory of one of the country's few genuine cannibals, a student lies down between two halves of an enormous loaf of bread and impersonates a human sandwich. There is also a Friends of Packer fan club. Some of its members even persuaded government officials at the Department of Agriculture to name a government cafeteria after Packer. Once they found out just who Packer was and what he ate, the government officials removed the name and the special plaque with his name on it. They said it was in "bad taste."

Far from the gold mines of Colorado and the cafeterias of Washington, but not too far from where Sir Ernest Shackleton and his men explored, there is something else that has tested man's ability to survive an ordeal. It's a narrow and deadly passage of water off the tip of South America called Cape Horn. Before the Panama Canal was built in 1914, it was the only way for ships to go from one side of North or South America to the other.

What makes the Cape so dangerous is the fact that powerful offshore winds force the sea through the narrow passage, creating killer storms, with rolling waves that have been known to rise over one hundred feet. For years fragile sailing ships took days, even weeks, to travel the few miles in this dangerous pass. Men were constantly swept overboard. Ships were crushed against rocks or icebergs.

The Panama Canal made it possible to avoid

this treacherous passage for most commercial ships, but there have always been sailors who have tried the Cape for the pure adventure of it. One of these was a Frenchman named Marcel Bardiaux. He had built a small sailboat in his backyard and wanted to try it out on a world cruise in 1952. In May of that year he nervously approached the Cape in his small boat.

There is never a good time to sail around the Cape. There are only bad times and not-so-bad times. Bardiaux decided to wait for a small break in the weather for a not-so-bad time. He had been fighting the winds and the currents for three days with no sleep and needed some sort of change of luck. Finally the seas calmed down and he was able to beach his boat on a sandbar and catch a short nap. While he slept the temperature dropped below freezing and his wet sails froze as stiff as plywood. To make them flexible enough to raise on his mast, he had to soak them in seawater. He had just set sail to begin his passage when an enormous wave came sweeping by and smashed into his tiny craft. It ripped the sails right off his mast, tore his small cabin shelter off the top of the boat, and washed away everything that was not tied or nailed down.

Fortunately Bardiaux had spare sails and was able to outfit his boat for another try. By then the weather had gotten worse and he was stranded out in the wild waters of the Cape. He already had frostbite from being out in the subfreezing temperatures and from constant soakings with sea water. He spent most of one day doing nothing but bailing water out of his small boat and trying to keep his hands from freezing solid. By the time he finished his work, his hands were aching from the cold and he could barely move them. And in spite of all his efforts he had barely progressed a foot farther than when he started to round the Cape days before. He headed for shore.

The weather was so bad he had to stay docked where he was for two days until he had what seemed like a good opportunity. But even after the weather seemed to improve it changed on him again after he set sail. The wind had turned against him, driving stinging hailstones and blinding sprays of icy sea water into his face. For two days and nights he struggled with his boat trying to fight his way through the storm, at one point throwing hot water, which he painstakingly boiled in a small kettle, to thaw out the ice-hardened canvas. Then, shortly after noon, five days after he had begun his passage around the Cape, Bardiaux finally saw what he had given up all hope of seeing, the Cape falling away behind him. He had completely passed around the Cape at last into calmer, safer, and warmer waters.

Five years later three British adventurers, Miles Smeeton, his wife Beryl, and a friend named John Guzzwell decided to round the same dangerous point of land, but going in the opposite direction from Bardiaux, west to east. That was supposed to be the "easy way" because the winds were less contrary that route. Even the easy way, they soon found, was not so easy.

They were in a slightly longer boat, a forty-two-foot ketch, and with three people managing things they expected to have a less difficult time than Bardiaux. Their first hint that they may have taken on more than they could handle was when they had to take in all their sails to keep them from getting ripped to shreds. Unlike Bardiaux, they were sailing with the winds, in what was supposed to be a safer course.

While they were roaring along in this "safe" course the powerful wind whipped up the sea into an even greater frenzy. The sea was so rough it caught the rear, or stern, of the boat and flipped it end over end. In spite of being tied to the boat by a lifeline, Beryl Smeeton found herself ripped off the deck and thrown into the surging, black sea. Her strong safety line was snapped as though it were nothing more than a rotten thread. Meanwhile, back on the boat, waves had broken off both masts and smashed away the roof of the cabin, filling it with water. A large hole was also bashed in the side of the yacht and it began sinking.

Amazingly, Mrs. Smeeton managed to swim back to the boat where her husband and John Guzzwell pulled her out of the water. Together they all managed to patch the hole in the side of the boat by nailing some extra sails and the door from a wooden locker over the hole. They bailed out as much water as they could, to keep afloat.

Right about then, their luck changed. The weather cleared for a moment, just long enough for the soaked crew to set a new course back to Chile and a dock where they could make repairs. The Cape Horn weather had beaten them back over one thousand miles and almost killed them, but they weren't ready to quit. As soon as the boat was seaworthy again they planned to make another try.

That came almost a year later when they set sail from the Chilean port and once again plotted a course for the deadly sea passage. This time they felt they were ready for the worst. And it was a good thing too, because the worst happened. The calm weather that moved with them for over a thousand miles suddenly and brutally changed. Once again the winds picked up and the sea began to rise and fall in an ominous roll. A day after they had started to slip around the Horn, a familiar disaster happened.

A gigantic wave rolled up on one side of the boat and completely flipped it over on its side. When it turned back upright, the hatches to the cabin had been pulled away and both masts were snapped off. Again they managed to rig up temporary sails so they could turn around and head back for Chile, this time for good. Twice they had tried the deadly passage the "easy" way, and each time the Cape almost killed them. They got away with their lives but unlike Monsieur Bardiaux and his small boat they did not manage to round the Horn.

Sailors like these went out and looked for their adventures. They knew ahead of time what they faced and were as prepared as they could be for what was coming. Not everyone has the luxury of being able to prepare for survival. Very often the challenge sneaks up when we least expect it.

This is what happened during World War II when an English ship, the S.S. Loumond was cruising the Atlantic Ocean and was hit by enemy torpedos. There were fifty-six crew members aboard. When the smoke from the explosion and fires drifted away minutes later, the ship had disappeared. With it went fifty-five of the crew. Only one man, a twenty-five-year-old Chinese seaman named Poon Lim, survived. When the torpedos hit, the explosion was so powerful it had literally blasted him out of his clothes and threw him into the water hundreds of yards away.

From where he drifted in the water he could see his ship quickly catch fire and just as suddenly sink down under the waves without a trace of any other survivors. He himself had to swim for more than two hours until he managed to snag a stray life raft that had broken loose from the ship. Scrambling on board he noticed the raft carried a supply of food and water. There looked to be enough to keep him fed until a passing ship spotted him and rescued him. So he began to wait.

A week came and went with no ship in sight. Then a month passed with agonizing slowness. Then it was two months and at the end of those sixty days he had to face a horrible truth. He was running out of food. Anything he needed to eat after that he knew he would have to get himself.

Since he was out there on the ocean, fish were the obvious choice for mealtimes, but how to catch them was the big question. He had no hook or bait. Taking apart the flashlight that came with the raft he pulled out the spring used to hold the batteries in place. After a little bending and twisting he was able to shape it into a crude hook which he attached to a line. With it he caught small fish that swam near his raft. Some of these he ate. Some he used as bait to entice larger fish to bite. A few times he even managed to snare an overly curious sea gull that came too close to his raft.

He lived like this for two more months, floating on the ocean with no notion of where he was going. Although he had no way of knowing it, the currents were slowly pushing him toward land, toward the coast of Brazil. At last, after more than four months alone out on the ocean — one hundred thirty-three days to be exact — his faded, weather-beaten raft was spotted by some Brazilian fishermen.

The man they saw was almost a human skeleton barely able to walk and, for a while, too stunned at being rescued to talk. For their part, the fishermen could not believe that such a small, frail-looking person could have survived drifting that long at sea. But there he was, living proof of man's will to survive under the worst possible conditions. The fishermen were impressed and in time so were many others, notably the king of England. When he heard of Poon Lim's amazing feat of endurance, he gave him the highest award the British government can bestow on anyone, the British Empire Medal. Even survival has its rewards.

Mark Fridley never got any medals for his feat of survival, but he probably doesn't care. The sixteen-year-old outdoorsman had picked out a real challenge for himself one day when hiking through Sequia National Park in California. He wanted to scale a tricky promontory named Moro Rock, seven thousand feet high, and he wanted to do it alone.

That turned out to be a big mistake, almost a fatal one. While partway up the sheer face of Moro Rock, he slipped and fell hundreds of feet to what should have been certain death.

For eleven days park rangers scoured the park on foot and in the air by helicopter. The search was turning up nothing, no signs or clues of any kind as to where young Fridley's body might have fallen. It looked like it was time to call off the search and give up the outdoorsman for dead. Maybe sometime in the future, they figured, a ranger or hiker might stumble across his remains, but there was no way they expected to find him alive now.

Hard to believe as it was, Mark was alive. At the time of his fall he broke both ankles, making him an instant cripple. When he realized he might be stuck in the woods for a while, he managed to pull himself over to where a small trickle of water was spilling over some rocks. That little bit of water, and the belief that he would eventually be rescued, were what kept him alive for eleven days.

There were times when his hopes and his strength were fading. More than once he would see an airplane or helicopter fly over and he would start waving and screaming only to see it move on without noticing him. In the end, however, his faith paid off. Giving the search one more try, the rangers finally found the crippled climber, emaciated, but very much alive, in the shadow of the rock that almost killed him.

Seven

Warnings About Death

Some people get a little extra help, when it comes to sidestepping death. It can come in many ways: as a hunch, a premonition that "something" is going to happen, as a dream, or even as a vision. There is no way of telling ahead of time which it will be. It varies from one person to the next. One thing all these warnings have in common is that they can make the difference between life and death and, more often than not, they defy all logical, scientific explanation.

Take one case mentioned by author Andrew McKenzie in his book *Riddle of the Future.* He tells about a British businessman named Jack Roberts who had flown to Bogotá, Colombia, with his fiancée, on a combined business and pleasure trip. While he was there some South American businessmen asked him to visit a factory about one hundred miles away. It was a short flight, they explained. They could go there and return the same day.

The next morning the plane took off, struggling

through the heavy cloud layer that blanketed the airport. An hour and a half later, when it had reached about nine thousand feet it crashed into a mountain, killing all aboard. Word flashed back to Bogotá and to the British embassy about the death of Mr. Roberts. British officials in turn notified his head office in London that he had died. In the meantime, embassy officials kept trying to call his fiancée's hotel room to break the sad news to her.

All day long there was no answer but later that night someone did manage to get through. When the phone was picked up Roberts himself answered it. Everyone was totally confused. Immediately the embassy notified London that Roberts was still very much alive. The reason was very odd.

The night before he was to make the plane trip, Roberts's fiancée had a dream in which a small plane crashed. She was convinced, she said, that was the plane he was to take and begged him not to go. Canceling a business trip because of a dream didn't make sense and he refused at first. But she kept insisting and even threatened to leave him if he went.

In the end, to humor her, he agreed, thinking she was upset about something and needed him to be there with her. He told the other businessmen he wouldn't be able to go. They at first suggested postponing the flight to another day, but when one of them insisted on leaving that morning they decided to stick to their original plans.

As it happened, the weather had already begun to look a little rough and Roberts was pleased to be spared what he suspected would be a bumpy airplane ride. Even the plane's pilot hesitated about going, not because of a dream, but because of a bad weather report. But the other businessmen insisted, so the plane left.

At the same time Roberts's fiancée insisted they go to church and pray for the safety of the plane's passengers. Roberts went along reluctantly to help ease her mind. He and the woman spent the better part of the day in church praying, not knowing that the plane had already crashed and that the embassy was frantically trying to call the hotel. When they returned to their hotel, they got the grim news. Roberts was shocked and totally surprised. But his fiancée wasn't.

As it happened, she had saved other lives before with her dreams when she was living with her mother in Germany during World War II. At one time they were settled in the city of Hamburg and during one night's sleep there, she had a dream which, she told her mother, was a sign that they had to move from where they were. When the mother asked why, the girl mysteriously said that their section of Hamburg "will not be here tomorrow." Although reluctant to move, the mother had seen her daughter's sense of the future work in the past and no longer questioned it. So they packed and moved to another part of the city. That night enemy bombers zoomed over the German metropolis and their bombs shattered a large part of Hamburg. The part where the woman and her mother lived was turned into acres of rubble.

It may not always be something as precise as a clear dream that helps certain people slip away from the grasp of death. All it may take sometimes is a vague premonition or an intuition of some kind that something violent is going to happen. One person who often had this extra sense of feeling out danger before it appeared was Winston Churchill, the famous prime minister of England. He had the chance to demonstrate it several times during World War II when the German Air Force was bombing the city of London.

As protection against the planes, antiaircraft guns were set up around the city to watch for and try to shoot down the German planes as they came in. Often ignoring the danger of the falling bombs, Churchill went around visiting these gun emplacements to encourage the soldiers manning them. One night in particular, after watching the gun crew blast away, he turned to get in his car. Suddenly he did a very strange thing. Instead of getting in and sitting on the side where he always sat, he walked all the way around to the opposite side of the car and sat there. Later, while being driven back to his office during the bombing attack, an enemy bomb hit a few feet away from his speeding car. It landed so close that the force of the impact rocked his car sideways, so that for a breathtaking second or two the car was traveling on only two wheels and seemed about to roll over. Fortunately, it didn't but instead, rocked back down and continued on. Churchill, who was a heavy man, said later it was probably his added weight on that side of the car — the side he had never sat on before — that kept it from overturning.

When his wife later asked him why he went to

all the trouble to change his seating arrangement on that particular night he explained: "Something said to me 'Stop!' before I reached the car door. It then appeared to me that I was told I was meant to open the door on the other side and get in and sit there — and that's what I did."

Another time during the war Churchill was having dinner with some of his government ministers. In those days business went on as usual while the bombing raids were going on.

This one night there was the usual air raid but Churchill's kitchen staff had been through it so many times they almost didn't hear the huge explosives roaring and thudding in the city. This one night, as they were preparing dinner, something seemed different, not to them, but to Churchill.

Without warning or explanation he rushed into the kitchen, told the butler to have the meal put on a hot plate in the dining room and then have the whole kitchen staff head for the bomb shelter. They followed his instruction and ran out. While they were sitting mystified in the bomb shelter, a stray bomb slammed into the house, totally destroying only one room, the kitchen.

Probably eeriest of all are the warnings that come from a person who no longer exists — or who maybe never existed. People who do not believe in ghosts find themselves face to face with something they could describe by no other name. Others who gave little or no thought to a world of helpful spirits get some rude, lifesaving awakenings that makes them pause and think.

Certainly Philadelphia doctor S. Weir Mitchell

wasn't thinking about ghosts or apparitions one evening as he sat in his home trying to relax after an exhausting day at the hospital. He had just begun to take a short nap when the jangling of his front doorbell woke him up.

When he opened the door a blast of frigid winter air blew in and there, standing on his front steps, was a skinny little girl. In spite of the cold, all she had on was a thin dress, a pair of beat-up, old shoes, and a ragged, old shawl that barely gave her any protection at all against the weather.

She said her mother was deathly ill and begged him to come and help her. Since he was a doctor, he could not refuse. He gathered up his medical bag, slipped into a heavy overcoat, and followed the girl through the dark streets of the city. The trail ended in a poor section of town at a drafty, rundown old building.

Leading the doctor up the rickety, rotting stairs, the little girl took him to a door and silently pointed to it. He knocked and stepped in. There, lying on the bed, he was surprised to see an old servant of his shivering and wrapped up in what bed covers she had.

She was very sick and probably would have died without medical help. The doctor examined her closely, found she had pneumonia, and ordered medicine for her to take. As he was finishing up his work and closing up his bag he mentioned to the woman that she was lucky to have such a brave and resourceful daughter who knew where to get a doctor so quickly.

The woman seemed totally startled by what he said. She told him that her only daughter had died just a month before and the only mementos left of her, she said, were in a small closet. Curious, the doctor opened the door and looked inside. There were a pair of scuffed shoes like the ones he had seen the girl wearing and also what looked like the same shawl.

Since it had been snowing that night it should have been a little wet from the weather. Gingerly the doctor laid his hand on the shawl. It was bone dry. He said no more about the girl, but as he was leaving the building he asked other people if they had seen the girl that came in with him or if they had seen any girl fitting that description around that night. No one had. In the end there was no possible explanation for whom or what the doctor saw, unless you believe in ghosts.

Ghosts, spirits, visions, or whatever you want to call them, are usually associated with past times and creaky old houses. But if you believe author John G. Fuller, helpful ghosts are still around today.

He spent months tracking down the story of the ghost of Flight 401 and wrote a book on the subject. An Eastern Airlines passenger plane crashed in the Florida Everglades in 1972, because a variety of small things went wrong. The landing gear seemed to get stuck and, as a crew member was inspecting it, the plane began to lose altitude gradually and ultimately crashed.

Over half those on board were killed. (You can read about how some people miraculously survived in Chapter Five.) The plane was almost, but not quite, totally destroyed. One part that remained amazingly intact was the galley section where the meals were cooked. There were a few other sections as well that somehow survived intact and worked fine. For this reason many of these working pieces were saved for use as replacement parts.

Eventually the usable bits and pieces of the plane that was Flight 401 ended up in other planes. And that was not all. Something, or someone, kept turning up in these same planes as well. It was an apparition of some kind that resembled Second Officer Don Repo, the man who had been trying to check the landing gear before the crash. There were rumors drifting around the airlines industry that he often showed up to warn the pilots and crew about possible trouble on board their planes. There was one pilot's story, for example, that a flight engineer sitting in his cockpit warned there was danger of an electrical failure. As an automatic precaution the pilot asked for another safety check on the airplane. It was done and it uncovered a faulty wire that could have shorted out and caused a fire. It was only later that the pilot realized who had given him that warning. It was the dead flight engineer from Flight 401.

Many of these visions or apparitions seemed to hover around one plane in particular, plane number 318. Over and over again stewardesses and other crew members kept seeing the face of Don Repo in one of the oven doors. It wasn't just a reflection or trick of the light because different stewardesses saw it at different times. It also wasn't anything that anyone could explain.

During the last time it was seen, the stewardess who spotted it grabbed another one and made her look as well to make sure she wasn't seeing things. When the other woman saw the man's face, they both went up to the cockpit and got the plane's flight engineer to come with them and make sure they weren't both going crazy.

The engineer saw the face too. What's more, he heard the face speak to him. Slowly and carefully it said to him, "Watch out for fire on this plane." The plane was on the way to Mexico City from New York City. It made it there with no problems.

After it had landed it turned out that one of the three engines needed major repair work that could not be done at Mexico City. So the airlines switched passengers to another plane and assigned a crew to fly the empty plane back to Miami for repairs. Even though only two of the three engines were working, the crew wasn't worried. The empty plane had more than enough power to get off the ground, even in the thin air of Mexico City where takeoffs are sometimes difficult. If only one engine was working, the crew would have a problem, however. One engine was just not strong enough to get them airborne.

The crew warmed up the plane and moved into takeoff position. Once he got the all-clear signal the pilot stepped up the power and began moving down the runway. In any plane's takeoff there is a critical point of no return. If the pilot has any sort of problems before that he can slow down the engines, turn around on the ground, and head back for the hangar. Once he gets past a certain speed he has no choice. He has to get the plane in the air or go down trying.

The taxiing went smoothly and the plane had just begun to lift off the ground, past this point of no return, when one of the engines began to buck and cough. It was skipping, losing power, and, worse, was in danger of catching fire. Immediately the pilot shut the engine off and turned on an automatic fire extinguisher. Then he struggled to get some more altitude — with only one engine.

Somehow, using what power was left in the one engine and all his piloting skills, he managed to keep climbing and got high enough and far enough away from the ground to breathe a little more easily. Later he got clearance to come back in for a landing. Those who were there the day of the near-accident were certain the plane would not make it. They were amazed at the pilot's good luck and skill. Later on, when the repair crew went to work on the engine that began to fail on takeoff, they were puzzled. They took the whole thing apart, down to the last bolt, and could find no reason why the engine suddenly flamed and quit when it did. There was no way that should have happened. But it did.

Stories about the ghostly flight engineer kept popping up over and over again. He turned up, the story went, only on airplanes that used pieces salvaged from crashed Flight 401. The oven doors on the Mexico City plane, for example, were from that plane. Although the airline that owned the airplanes never admitted they believed in this airborne ghost, in time they quietly took Flight 401's salvaged parts off their planes. As they did the man's ghost and the stories about him slowly faded away.

In legends and stories of the occult, probably the strangest is the notion of what is called the *Doppelganger*, a German term for a kind of spirit that is an exact double of the person who sees it. By tradition the *Doppelganger* is not a semitransparent ghost that you can see through, but someone or something that looks exactly like a real, solid person with one important distinction. Very often it appears as a pale bloodless version of yourself, almost like looking at yourself as a corpse.

Generally the *Doppelganger* shows up for a couple of reasons. Sometimes it shows up as a symbol of the conflict going on in a person's soul. There are legends about a human doing battle with and killing a mysterious stranger. When he rips off the mask he sees not a stranger, but himself. A *Doppelganger* also may appear as some sort of warning of danger.

Psychic expert John Godwin tells about one *Doppelganger* in his book *The Unsolved World of the Unknown.* The story begins on a back country road in France in World War II and ends on a hiking trail in Canada years later. During the war a man named Alex Griffith, a sergeant in the American infantry, was out on a patrol. It was a warm, balmy day, completely peaceful. It was hard to believe there was still a war going on in the cool green hills around where he and his men were patrolling.

Griffith was walking along in a kind of pleasant daze taking in the surroundings and not really paying as close attention to possible dangers as he should have. But when he raised his eyes to search a stretch of dirt road ahead, he came alert instantly when he saw another American soldier, a sergeant, standing in the middle of the road waving. He couldn't hear the man but he understood well enough what the waving was supposed to mean: Turn back! Turn back! The next shock came when he realized who the soldier was. It was Griffith himself, same beard growth, same dirty uniform, and even the same Band-Aid covering a small cut on his face.

Instinctively Griffith turned and ordered his men off the road. When he looked again to see what had happened to his mirror image it was gone.

The soldiers had obeyed him instantly. He and his squad had moved several hundred yards down the road and regrouped. The men stood patiently waiting for an explanation for his abrupt order and some clue as to what to do next.

Griffith walked toward them wondering what to say. What was he going to tell them? That he had seen his exact double and they were all going to follow his double's orders? It sounded crazy. To kill some time he lit a cigarette. He noticed that his hands were shaking.

He was about to speak when a jeep with two Americans went roaring past him. It sped up the road and past the point where they had turned back. In a matter of seconds Griffith discovered why he had stopped his men. He heard a faraway stuttering noise. He recognized it instantly as a heavy machine gun. He sent someone to see what had happened. The jeep had driven straight into a

German ambush. A machine gun nest was cleverly hidden around the bend in the road. Had Griffith and his men wandered into that same spot, they would have been cut down in a matter of seconds.

More than twenty years passed. Griffith had settled down in the Midwest where he became a successful business executive. One year on vacation he, his wife, and his two children went camping in the province of Quebec. Out hiking one day they were surprised by a sudden storm. The undergrowth was thick and the trail narrow, so the family lined up single file as they made their way back to the campsite, with Mrs. Griffith in the rear and her husband in the lead.

A strong wind had begun to rock the trees, and bits and pieces of branches had begun raining down on them. Griffith searched ahead for the trail. The trees thinned out a little and he spotted a clearing not far away. When he took a second look he was momentarily surprised to see a man standing in it.

With a sudden shock Griffith realized what he was seeing. A few yards away was a man in the combat uniform of a World War II American soldier. He was a sergeant, had a few days growth of beard on his face, and a Band-Aid on his chin. Griffith, in shock, saw himself as he looked in war twenty years before. His *Doppelganger* shouted to him but again Griffith could hear nothing. The mouth of this eerie figure moved but no words came out. The figure waved at him. The message was clear: Turn back!

Instantly Griffith turned to his family behind him and shouted in terror: Back! As his family turned back along the path he looked back at the clearing and saw nothing and no one. Not more than five seconds later he heard a sharp crack and a sickening crash. The ground around his feet vibrated as though a small bomb had been set off.

The whole area of the clearing was filled with dust. At first it was hard to see what had happened. Once the dust settled, it all became clear. The strong winds apparently were too much for an enormous old tree. The gusts toppled it over so that it smashed to the ground precisely where Alex Griffith and his family would have been standing if they had taken a few more steps. The sergeant had disappeared.

Since then he has not seen any sign of that mysterious World War II soldier and his Band-Aid patched chin, but one thing is certain, when he does show up he will get Alex Griffith's full attention. In all probability his life will depend on it.

Eight

The Deaths That Never Were

There is probably nothing stranger and more curious than a non-death, the kind that happens only in people's minds, when someone is declared dead while being very much alive. Sometimes, these people "die" because of some misunderstanding. Sometimes, they are the casualty of some kind of confusion. Or sometimes, they are done in by a bad joke.

What is probably one of the best-known cases of a living person who didn't die — even though everyone else thought he did — happened in England in the 1700s to a man named John Partridge. He had made an enemy of the British writer Jonathan Swift, the man who wrote *Gulliver's Travels*. Swift decided that one day he would get rid of Partridge, as bloodlessly as possible.

Under the fake name of Isaac Bickerstaff, Swift wrote a pamphlet called *Predictions for the Year 1708*. Among the predictions he made was that a certain man named John Partridge would mysteriously die on March 29 of that year.

When Partridge read this he was furious and tried to find out who this Bickerstaff character was. He never did. After a while he completely forgot about what he thought was nothing more than a bad joke. He went back to his work, publishing a magazine that was widely read in the London of his day.

March 29 of 1708 arrived and found John Partridge very much alive and healthy. He assumed everyone had forgotten about the ridiculous prediction that had been made the previous year. Everyone had except for one person, Jonathan Swift, the man who made it to begin with.

On March 30 Swift sat down at his desk and, using another assumed name, wrote an article in which he said that, true to the prediction of that amazing Mr. Bickerstaff, poor Mr. John Partridge died yesterday. People who read Swift's article were tremendously impressed by the prediction's accuracy. Some were even a little sad to read about the passing of Mr. Partridge.

In the meantime, Partridge was still alive and well, although more and more people were beginning to doubt that. To complicate his situation there was a rumor going around London that the magazine which had been published by the now-deceased Mr. Partridge had been taken over by a fraud who continued to use the dead man's name. That rumor was planted by Jonathan Swift as well.

Soon Partridge found that his regular readers believed the rumor and had stopped buying his magazine. All but his closest friends had assumed he had died, as predicted. In the end, business was so bad he had to sell the magazine. Through it all he never did manage to find out who it was who had really "killed" him. He was probably the first victim ever buried alive by a bad joke.

In the 1800s the whole human race got a reprieve from destruction. It had been predicted by a farmer who became a preacher. The man's name was William Miller. He had studied the Bible for years and, after some special interpretation of his own, decided that there was a distinct message hidden there giving the precise date when the world would end. After a little complicated arithmetic, he decided the Bible set the date of the end of the world for some time in 1843.

Miller became widely known as a persuasive preacher and he soon began to attract a loyal following. Word of his prediction spread and at one point a New York City newspaper ran a story saying that, according to Miller, the world would end in flames on April 13, 1843. Many of his believers got ready. They gathered together on hilltops all over New England and waited patiently for the end to come. Many sold everything they owned so they would have nothing to take to heaven. Others dressed in shrouds in preparation for the end.

April 13 came. And it went. Life in the world went on very much as it did before. Miller himself later admitted that his arithmetic must have been wrong, but added that the end would definitely come sometime before April 1844.

Several dates before then were predicted as end-of-the-world days. Each time his followers got themselves ready and waited patiently. Some climbed trees or hilltops so they would be closer to heaven when the end came or, in some instances, gathered in graveyards where they could mingle with the crowds of souls rising from the dead. Each time was like the one before. Nothing happened.

The Millerites, as these believers came to be called, started to be the butt of jokes and pranksters. On one of these predicted judgment days a practical joker sneaked up outside a Millerite prayer hall and blew a loud trumpet. The believers inside, thinking it was an angel, shouted, "Hallelujah, the time has come!" The horn-blower shouted back, "No, it hasn't, you fools," and ran off howling with laughter.

Things looked bad for Miller, especially when his last possible date for the end of the world, March 31 of 1844, came and went without anything happening. Not a man to be easily discouraged, he did some more recalculating and decided the true date when the world would definitely end in flames was October 22, 1844.

If people were frantic before, they were absolutely hysterical now. When the day came several people again put on long white robes so they would fit in with the heavenly choir. One farmer even brought his cows along and put white robes on them. He said they would be used to provide milk for the children on the way to heaven. "It's a long trip," he explained.

The sun rose on October 22. People all over the United States waited nervously, many getting stiff necks from constantly staring up at the sky for the first sign from the heavens. The day dragged on and on. Children fidgeted and cried.

The adults milled around getting more and more restless and impatient. Some expected the end to come at the first light of day. When the sun rose and nothing happened, others started guessing that maybe it would all happen at noon or at the end of the day. But the sun set as usual. Nothing happened. Others assumed it had to be at the stroke of midnight. And so they waited.

Midnight came and went, uneventfully. The Millerites finally had to admit their leader was wrong, again. Disappointed and heartbroken, they went home. After that William Miller never made another prediction, although many of his followers remained loyal to him and his other teachings. Since that time followers of Miller's preachings have referred to that October day in 1844 as The Disappointment.

There have always been times when religious leaders and preachers of one kind or another have used the image of death, the end of your life or someone else's, to deliver some kind of religious message. William Miller and his followers were certain they would all die on that disappointing October day more than one hundred years ago. And in December of 1979 some Christmas shoppers in the town of Lawton, Oklahoma, were equally certain that somewhere in their town there was the body of a man in a local department store.

For days the local police, newspapers, and radio stations were getting telephone calls telling them to look for the body of a man under the gift wrapping counter of one or another of the local department stores. The story was that he had slipped and fallen to the floor where he died. In their pre-Christmas frenzy to get their gifts wrapped, shoppers callously stepped over him. Eventually his body was nudged out of sight under a counter and abandoned there.

Police and reporters were frantically trying to locate the store and the body of this unfortunate person. After days of searching, the truth about the dead man and the department store finally came out. It began with a Sunday sermon preached by the Reverend Forrest Siler, a local Baptist minister. He was trying to make a point of how people often forget the spiritual side of Christmas in all the commercial promotion that goes on at the time of year. To make the story more impressive he began by telling them a modern parable of a quiet man standing in a crowd of Christmas shoppers as they pressed in on a gift wrapping counter. The man stood there silently with no gift in his hands to wrap. One by one people shoved him aside until finally he fell over and was pushed under the counter where he died of neglect. The man, it was found later, had unusual scars on the palms of his hands, scars from having been crucified.

The man, of course, was supposed to be Christ and the idea was that here all these people were too caught up in Christmas buying to pay any attention to the real Christ standing right there among them. This was the parable, the story with a lesson, that the minister was trying to tell. However, people seemed to forget the parable and only remember the story itself. And so the rumor about the dead man began. After all the confusion about the dead man was finally cleared up, the minister concluded he probably overdid the story part a little too much.

Make-believe deaths like this happen every now and then in the form of what some people call modern legends. Stories get started and, even though they are not true, they get spread around by word of mouth, maybe even picked up by newspapers and reported as fact.

They can be about almost anything to do with death. Some are about people dying of weird causes. For example, a few years ago one popular story claimed that if you ate a fizzy candy too fast, your stomach would explode and you'd die. Another claimed that a certain brand of bubble gum had spider eggs inside. Both stories were not true, but for a long time it was hard to convince kids it was all right to eat them.

Probably the strangest of these modern stories, according to legend hunter Professor Jan Harold Brunvald of the University of Utah, is the one you could call the "Snake in the Fur Coat." It begins with a woman visiting a store that is having a big sale on fur coats. There are racks and racks of them, all imported from Mexico.

She finds a coat in her size she likes and tries it on. As she slips one hand in a pocket she feels a sharp stabbing pain in one of her fingers. Quickly she pulls it out and looks at it. There are two small puncture wounds in it. As she is standing there trying to figure out what happened she feels something moving in the coat. When she looks down she sees a long green snake slither out of the pocket, drop to the floor, and crawl away.

Screaming with fear and horror the woman tries to rip of the coat and finds that her arm is already beginning to throb, swelling up, and turning black and blue. The store calls an ambulance which rushes her to the hospital. The poison is working fast. The doctors have to decide what to do, so they cut off her arm to keep the poison from spreading. It's too late. The woman dies anyway.

According to Brunvand this story has surfaced in different forms all over the country and is always untrue, always a rumor. After it appeared in a Texas newspaper, for example, a reporter investigating the story called the hospital where the woman supposedly died. They had no record of any such patient. He called the doctor who supposedly cut off her arm. The doctor said he had heard the story but hadn't actually handled the case. The reporter tried the police and health department. They had never heard of a poisonous fur coat attacking anyone.

After many phone calls the reporter finally managed to get the name of the woman who was bitten. He then called her home. She answered the phone. He asked how she felt. Fine, she said, and wondered why he was calling. The reporter explained the whole story about the snake in the fur coat. It wasn't me, the woman said but she added that she had also heard the story, only it didn't involve a fur coat. It had to do with a woman who was shopping and who was bitten by a snake. This snake was hiding in a fruit basket. The reporter never did find a trace of the snake, the deadly fur coat, or any woman who supposedly had tried it on and had been bitten. The whole thing was pure fiction.

Rumors and incorrect facts have almost killed off more than one person, as one woman named Mavis McIntosh found out a few years ago. In her work, McIntosh represented many famous writers, among them John Steinbeck. It happened that someone who had written a biography of John Steinbeck mentioned McIntosh in his book and made the mistake of saying that she was dead. She was not.

Shortly after the book came out, McIntosh started noticing that many of her old friends stopped calling her. She began asking around and soon found out it was because they thought she had died. After hearing that, she got in touch of the man who wrote the biography and his publisher and told them to change the book to read that she was still alive.

They did but they also made another mistake. The book said she was alive, but had stopped working. Now, some people thought she was dead. And others thought she was not working anymore. There was more confusion. Her clients stopped calling her because they thought she was out of business. Totally fed up with another mistake, McIntosh got a lawyer and sued the author and publisher for one hundred thousand dollars because of their carelessness with the facts. As her lawyer put it, "To read about your death is pretty upsetting."

It is even more disturbing to be told straight to your face that you are dead. One woman in Tacoma, Washington, had this happen after she left her house to go out for lunch and came back to a nasty surprise. When Victoria Carlbom went to open her front door she noticed something new had been added in the short time she was away. The door was boarded up and padlocked. Not only that, her dog, Sissy-Poo, was missing. Thoroughly upset she went to the nearest telephone and called the police.

The officer on duty checked the records. He asked if this was the house that belonged to Victoria Carlbom. She said it was. Well, the police officer explained, they had a report that Victoria Carlbom had committed suicide. To protect the home and its contents they stopped by, boarded up the building, and took her dog to the dog pound. When she asked how they knew Victoria Carlbom had committed suicide he said someone had called the department earlier in the day to report the death.

Mrs. Carlbom pointed out that the police were mistaken. When the policeman asked how she knew, she said that *she* was Victoria Carlbom and was very much alive. She also wanted to get her dog back and get into her house. The police told her they had no key.

So she had to break a window to get into her own house. Not only that but when she went to the dog pound, officials there told her it would cost five dollars to get Sissy-Poo back. Who it was who called and reported her "suicide" to the police she never found out, although she suspected it was someone she described as a "slightly off-balance friend."

Another case of what you might call a mistaken death happened in the wake of a car crash in Virginia. The facts of the case are clear—up to a point.

One night on a road in Virginia there was a two-car accident. It was a huge wreck. Rescuers worked hard to get the people out, but for four of the seven people involved it was too late. The police had the sad duty of calling up the families of those who were in the crash to ask them to come down and identify the bodies of the victims.

Among those called were the parents of Kathy Storey. They were shown a young girl believed to be their 21-year-old daughter. The car crash had been so violent it disfigured her face. Still, the family saw enough to identify Kathy. Sadly, they planned funeral services for the girl and had her remains cremated.

In the meantime one of the other accident victims who survived, a girl named Alana, had been unconscious for three days because of her injuries. When she woke up one of the police officers investigating the accident came in to talk to her.

"Alana, I'm here to interview you about the accident you were involved in."

The woman looked confused. "My name is Kathy," she said.

This time it was the police officer's turn to be confused. "Aren't you Alana?" he asked.

"My name is Kathy Storey," she said.

It was shortly after this that the police noticed some other features that didn't belong to Alana.

Alana didn't have pierced ears, for example. Kathy did. After checking more carefully, the police telephoned Kathy's parents, who were stunned to learn that their daughter was not dead after all. They, of course, were ecstatic as well as surprised.

The police were also left with the job of telling the family of the other girl, Alana, the sad news about the mistake. All were sad and everyone was shocked, except for Alana's brother who said, "I had a sixth sense she wasn't my sister." His sixth sense, sadly, was right.

In the end there is no non-death as final as being officially non-existent. A 50-year-old man named Robert Petee found this out in a very strange way. In 1951, Petee was a soldier in the U.S. Army, a job he didn't like very much. Rather than return to his base one day, he decided to hide out in the apartment of a German friend. He stayed there for 28 years, from 1951 to 1979. His family in the meantime gave him up for dead.

Eventually his conscience got the better of him and he turned himself over to Army authorities. Since his 28 years in hiding had left him a nervous and broken man, the Army decided not to punish him.

Petee returned home to Michigan, but he'd been away so long, few remembered him. He drifted around working odd jobs and trying to settle down in a country he hadn't seen in more than a quarter of a century. As much as he tried, he just couldn't get comfortable. He missed Germany; so after two years of trying to be an American again, he gave up and decided to return to the adopted country he had actually come to know better.

That turned out not to be as easy as he had hoped. To get a passport he, like any American citizen, had to produce some proof that he was born in this country or some proof of citizenship. When he went to the records office in his home town to get that, he faced an odd problem. County authorities there looked but couldn't find any trace of birth records for Petee. He not only was someone who had been considered dead for many years, but, in official eyes at any rate, he also had the bizarre distinction of being somebody who had never been born.